THE MONROE DOCTRINE

THE
MONROE DOCTRINE

Edited by ARMIN RAPPAPORT

University of California, Berkeley

HOLT, RINEHART AND WINSTON
New York • Chicago • San Francisco • Toronto • London

CONTENTS

INTRODUCTION

In 1815, after the defeat of Napoleon, the victorious powers, England, Russia, Prussia, and Austria, joined together in the Quadruple Alliance to preserve the postwar settlement agreed to at the Congress of Vienna. In the same year the Tsar of Russia created the Holy Alliance, which included all the sovereigns of Europe except the Pope, the Sultan of Turkey, and the British monarch. This alliance was not a formal political or military agreement but a pledge taken by the signatories to conduct their affairs according to the precepts of "justice, Christian charity, and peace." Many contemporary observers and later historians used interchangeably the terms "Quadruple Alliance" and "Holy Alliance" but it was only the Quadruple Alliance that was the official agency for maintaining the European settlement.

The principal objective of the Quadruple Alliance was to prevent revolution from once again convulsing France and thereby disturbing the peace of Europe. It soon became clear, however, that France under the restored Bourbons had become a reliable, stable, and dependable nation. In fact, by 1818 France was admitted into the "concert of Europe," whereupon the Quadruple became the Quintuple Alliance.

But if France was safe from upheaval, much of the rest of Europe was not. Revolutions broke out in Greece, Portugal, Spain, and Italy and the allies, at a series of conferences, took measures to suppress them. Austria was designated to send an expedition to quell a revolt in Italy and a French army was dispatched to put one down in Spain.

Suppression of the revolution in Spain and restoration of the deposed king, Ferdinand VII, led quite naturally to a movement to restore Ferdinand's authority in the Spanish colonies in the Western Hemisphere where revolutions had broken out. The revolts, begun in 1808 as a protest against Napoleon's action in placing his brother on the Spanish throne, were transformed into wars for independence after the defeat of the French Emperor. By 1822, all the mainland colonies had been successful in ending Spanish rule, and there was talk in Europe that year of convening a congress to plan an expedition under French leadership to reassert Spanish authority in these former colonies.

1

At the same time, another event was taking place which affected the Western Hemisphere. In September 1821 the Russian Tsar issued a decree in which he laid claim to the west coast of North America down to 51 degrees (the present Canadian-American boundary is at 49 degrees) and ordered all foreign vessels to keep a distance of one hundred miles from the coast.

To both these situations, Great Britain objected strongly. For one thing, the Tsar's decree impinged on territory claimed by Britain. More important, however, was the threat of Spain's regaining its former colonies. The newly independent republics of South America had opened their ports to ships of all nations and the British were engaging in a profitable trade which had hitherto been a Spanish monopoly. A restoration of Ferdinand's authority would surely lead to a revival of Spanish restrictive commercial practices and shut Britain out of the Latin-American markets. And finally, reconquest of the former colonies by a French-led expedition would add to French strength and prestige in Europe and America.

Such was the state of international affairs when on December 2, 1823, President Monroe sent to Congress his seventh annual message, which covered various aspects of the nation's life. He noted the state of the army and navy, commented on the development of roads and canals, surveyed the explorations in the West, reported on financial and economic conditions, and mentioned the efforts being made to settle disputes with Great Britain and France.

But imbedded in this factual report were two statements of general principles in widely separated paragraphs: (1) ". . . the American continents, by the free and independent conditions which they have assumed and maintain, are henceforth not to be considered as subjects for future colonization by any European powers." (2) "The political system of the [European] allied powers is essentially different . . . from that of America. . . . We owe it, therefore, to candor and to the amicable relations existing between the United States and those powers to declare that we should consider any attempt on their part to extend their system to any portion of this hemisphere as dangerous to our peace and safety." Taken together, these two ideas—noncolonization and separation of the two hemispheres—constitute the Monroe Doctrine.

Historians agree that at the time of enunciation the Doctrine had no effect on the European powers and that the United States had neither the strength nor the inclination to enforce it. They agree, too, that by the start of the twentieth century the Doctrine had reached the point where it was respected and feared by the nations of the world because the United States had both the will and the might to enforce it. By that time, it had developed into one of the basic and fundamental precepts of American foreign policy, revered and respected by all factions, sections, and political parties.

Historians differ, however, on other aspects of the Doctrine and this pamphlet explores the differences by presenting extracts from the principal books and articles on the subject. A student examining the controversial literature may well wonder why historians diverge in their interpretations of an event in the past. Are not the facts "factual"? Did not the event take place? The student must, of course, realize that while there may be no question but that a certain event occurred, the reasons, motives, and causes for its happening are not as certain. Everybody agrees that President Monroe delivered a message to Congress and stated certain principles but the reasons why he made the statement and the source of the principles are not so indisputable. Historians examining precisely the same evidence may, and do, come up with completely different answers. Their answers depend entirely on how they view the raw material: the weight they assign to a phrase or statement, the importance they ascribe to an event, or the credibility they give to an assertion. And how they view the raw material in turn depends on their own frame of reference.

Scholars who have written on the Monroe Doctrine have, for the most part, used much the same source material—the writings of James Monroe, John Quincy Adams, Henry Clay, George Canning, and other participants, as well as the diplomatic correspondence of the principal powers, the United States, Great Britain, France, and Russia. Still, their answers to the basic questions are different.

The first problem raised here concerns the circumstances that gave rise to the Doctrine and its purpose, that is, why it was enunciated when it was and what it was expected to accomplish. Three conflicting points of view are presented. In the first selection, Dexter Perkins claims that it developed as a consequence of European events in the autumn of 1823. For him, the Doctrine was a response to the advance of the Russians down the west coast of North America into territory claimed by the United States and the threat by the Continental powers to reconquer the Spanish colonies in the New World. To ward off these twin dangers, President Monroe issued his warning, and it was directed against the would-be transgressors.

Edward H. Tatum, Jr., challenges this thesis. While he admits that the events of the last months of 1823 brought the Doctrine into being, he maintains that the message embodies ideas and attitudes common in the United States before 1823 and that these were chiefly anti-British rather than anti-Continental powers. For Tatum, the Doctrine must be viewed in the light of long-standing distrust in the United States of British ambitions in the Western Hemisphere. The Doctrine then becomes an expression of a deep-seated feeling crystallized by the particular occurrences in 1823.

A critical examination of the text of the message in this framework led Tatum to conclude that the two parts of the Doctrine were directed against

Great Britain. He believes that neither Adams nor Monroe feared the designs of the Continental powers in the New World; indeed, they recognized that the menace from those quarters was a British fabrication. What troubled them was not the Russian plan to colonize the west coast of North America but Britain's designs on Cuba; not the danger of reconquest of the Spanish colonies by the Continental nations but the extension of British monopolistic practices to the New World.

Why should the difference in interpretation be so great? Is there any significance in the fact that Perkins wrote in the mid-1920s and Tatum a decade later or that Perkins lived on the east coast of the United States (closer to Europe) while Tatum worked in California (remote from the Old World)? Does Tatum overrate Anglo-American hostility? Does Perkins focus too narrowly upon the official diplomatic events and ignore public attitudes? Does he put too much credence in Anglo-American cordiality? How do the two authors diverge in their assessment of the crucial Rush-Canning conversations as a prelude to the pronouncement of the Doctrine?

Arthur P. Whitaker, an authority on Latin America, in the third selection takes issue with both Perkins and Tatum. On the subject of American hostility toward Great Britain, he supports Tatum and, indeed, adds important new evidence, but he remarks, "this is not to say that Monroe was induced . . . to aim his declaration against Britain. . . ." Whitaker takes the position that Monroe directed his message chiefly against France, the nation which alone had the capability and the inclination to lead an invasion of South America, which George Canning, the British foreign secretary, feared as the chief rival to Great Britain in the New World, and which Monroe singled out in a statement to a Latin-American diplomat as the target of his warning. He does not eliminate other European nations from the scope of the Doctrine and subscribes to the view that Monroe and Adams certainly had Russia in mind and probably any other nation that had pretensions to American territory. Is Whitaker's reliance on Monroe's conversation with the Latin-American diplomat sufficient basis for his conclusion?

The second problem deals with authorship. Whose ideas did the message reflect? Who was responsible for the language, the form, the occasion for enunciation? Almost every important American statesman and politician of the time has been given credit for the authorship by some historian. Even Canning has had an advocate. The most serious contenders for the honor, however, are Thomas Jefferson, James Monroe, and John Quincy Adams.

The earliest scholarly claim was made on behalf of John Quincy Adams by Worthington C. Ford. While the President and his cabinet vacillated, it was Adams who proposed a vigorous reply to Canning's suggestion for joint overtures and to the autocratic and despotic principles expressed by the

Russian Tsar. Ford concludes that it was Adams who drafted the reply in language boldly proclaiming the virtues of republicanism and the separation of Europe from America. Ford's case rests on the belief that Adams' ideas and drafts became Monroe's message with very little change. Is Ford's case sufficient to justify his conclusion that "it is enough to follow the course of events . . . to know that the Monroe Doctrine was the work of John Quincy Adams"?

While Ford emphasizes the immediate events in the fall of 1823 in crediting Adams with the authorship of the Doctrine, T. R. Schellenberg points to the more general principles lying behind the message in stressing Thomas Jefferson's contribution. He concedes that Adams was responsible for the noncolonization clause but maintains that we are indebted to Jefferson for the more significant idea of the "two spheres," that is, the separation of Europe and America.

What is Schellenberg's evidence for the high place assigned to the third president? It is Jefferson's long-term interest in America's steering clear of Europe and, more important, his reading of de Pradt. But might not Adams have read de Pradt? Can it be said with any degree of certainty that de Pradt added anything to the climate already existing in the United States (and dating back to the earliest days of the republic) for separation from Europe? Is there not an excess of conjecture in Schellenberg's argument? Is he convincing in his estimate of the extent of Monroe's reliance on Jefferson for advice?

In Schellenberg's analysis, President Monroe has a slight place. William A. MacCorkle, using the same sources as Ford and Schellenberg ascribes to Monroe the principal credit for grasping firmly all the problems connected with South American affairs and for stating the American position on those matters. For MacCorkle, it is Monroe who had all the ideas and all the determination necessary for the Doctrine. But does it seem reasonable that Adams, certainly no less strong and the President's adviser on foreign affairs, should have played no part in directing the chief executive's thoughts? Does MacCorkle's analysis focus too narrowly on Monroe to the exclusion of other possible sources of influence in formulating the message?

The third problem is concerned with Britain's suggestions in the summer and fall of 1823 for a joint Anglo-American declaration to ward off the projected Continental expedition to South America and the American response. The importance of this problem lies in the relationship between the overtures and the enunciation of the Doctrine. It was the concern felt by George Canning, British foreign secretary from 1822 to 1827, about the plans of the Continental powers to invade the former Spanish colonies and about the Russian move in North America which prompted his inquiry to the American minister, Richard Rush, in August 1823, as to the possibility of a joint pronouncement. And it was his interview with Rush that stimulated discussions in Washington which, in turn, led to the declaration by Monroe. As C. K. Webster, the British historian, has pointed out, "Canning provided the occasion and opportunity for expounding those very sentiments [the Monroe Doctrine] and had he not made his offer to Rush, it seems unlikely that any declaration about America would have been made in the form of Monroe's message."

On the question of Canning's motives for soliciting American cooperation for a joint declaration, there are two principal theses. William W. Kaufmann examines the European situation and Britain's position in the post-Napoleonic world and concludes that Canning sought American support to immobilize the Continental alliance. For Kaufmann, Canning's motives were purely political and diplomatic. He acted out of consideration for the balance of power. From Kaufmann's account it would appear that no other influences operated on the British foreign secretary. What about public opinion? What of the pressures of various groups in England? What of economic considerations?

That such pressures were present is reflected in the selection by George Dangerfield. For him the key to Canning's courtship of the young republic across the ocean lay in the desire of the rising British manufacturing class to capture the American market. Friend of William Huskisson and other free traders and himself an opponent of the old mercantilist empire, Canning pursued policies designed to expand markets overseas. To invite the United States to join Britain was to flatter and conciliate the Americans thereby making them agreeable to receiving British manufactures by a reduction of the tariff. The United States was, after all, the great market. Does Dangerfield's economic interpretation extend to an implication that John Quincy Adams' earlier overtures to Canning were rooted in his wish to gain greater trade rights for Americans in British colonial ports? Dangerfield does not eliminate factors other than economic as Canning's motivation but he believes that the paramount reason for the foreign secretary's flirtation was that he was the "unconscious servant of British coal and iron, of British spindles and furnaces." Does he rely too heavily on "unconscious" pressures? Can such pressures be weighed? Can their effect be measured?

As for the American response to Canning's overtures, did Monroe and Adams by their unilateral pronouncement close the door to any future Anglo-American remonstrances? Until Gale W. McGee's researches, the answer to this question had always been in the affirmative. The Doctrine had been viewed as an isolationist statement. His investigations, however, led to his concluding that the idea of combining policies with Great Britain was always present in calculations of Monroe and Adams and was not abandoned after December 2, 1823. Despite their reluctance to involve the United States in European affairs, the security of their country led them to keep open the line between London and Washington. Because one day Britain's assistance might be useful or necessary, the two American statesmen "stood ever ready to compromise ideals [isolationism] with the exigencies of reality." Do Monroe's remarks and observations justify McGee's view that the President issued the Doctrine only as a "stopgap measure"?

The final problem deals with an evaluation of the Doctrine. Two principal questions are considered: what did Latin Americans think of Monroe's message and has the message any validity today? Generally speaking, Latin Americans have viewed the Doctrine with hostility. Some have considered it pernicious from the very beginning; others have maintained that it became bad only because of its development in the nineteenth and twentieth centuries by means of corollaries and through interpretations which served as a cloak for United States aggression. Since its enunciation in 1823, the Doctrine has been subject to numerous and various interpretations by successive presidents and secretaries of state which, in some instances, could have been viewed by Latin Americans as justification for exerting hegemony in the hemisphere.

Henry Clay's statement in 1825 that neither Cuba nor Porto Rico could be transferred to any other power by Spain came to be known as the "no-transfer corollary" and was reiterated by other United States officials in later years. President James K. Polk in 1845 advanced a "Polk Corollary," which declared that "no future European colony or dominion . . . be planted or established on any part of the North American continent." In 1895, Secretary of State Richard Olney proclaimed, "The United States is practically sovereign on this continent, and its fiat is law. . . ." Finally, in 1904, Theodore Roosevelt in the "Roosevelt Corollary" announced that the United States would intervene in the domestic affairs of any Latin American republic in "flagrant cases of wrongdoing."

Gaston Nerval is the most eloquent and convincing representative of the point of view that the Doctrine was pernicious from the beginning. The motive of the United States in enunciating the Doctrine, he states, was "to protect the safety and peculiar interests of the country which sponsored it" and not to help the newly liberated republics. Not knowing Monroe's purposes, South American diplomats journeyed to Washington to seek United States aid for implementing the Doctrine. They were rebuffed. Here, says Nerval, is proof that the "original Monroe Doctrine was a *unilateral, egoistic policy and exclusively of the United States.*" Is he fair in this judgment? Should the United States have been expected to bind itself by commitments to Latin American states?

Luis Quintanilla disagrees with Nerval's view of the Doctrine when it was first pronounced. For him, it was mild "at the outset; a candid but commendable United States gesture against European interference." Subsequently, however, as a consequence of corollaries and interpretations, it became "a ruthless axiom" and "Machiavellian." Quintanilla lists the most damaging additions to the Doctrine as those made by Henry Clay, James K. Polk, Richard Olney, and Theodore Roosevelt. Each, he claims, served to extend United States hegemony and curtail the sovereignty of the southern republics. Note the five charges he makes against the Doctrine. Can any of them be refuted using material in the preceding selections? Are any of them valid even from the point of view of the United States? In his final indictment, Quintanilla states that the Doctrine has become outmoded. With the world moving to collective security and international cooperation, there is no longer room for one nation to determine the destinies of a whole continent. The Doctrine may not be dead, he states, "but there is little use for it today."

As might be expected, a Soviet interpretation of the Doctrine is extremely hostile. S. Gonionsky goes beyond Quintanilla in insisting that the Doctrine is dead because the nations of the Western Hemisphere are demanding independence from the United States and will no longer accept direction from the "imperialist" giant of the north. Gonionsky's views and the terms he uses are typical of Soviet historical writing. The terms "ruling class," "interventionist design," and "aggressive and two-faced policy" are used to characterize United States motives and actions. It is not strange that Gonionsky castigates the Doctrine, for it may be the instrument for frustrating Soviet designs on the Western Hemisphere.

An American affirmation of faith in Monroe's message is the substance of the last selection. In it, Raymond Moley presents a refutation of both Quintanilla and Gonionsky. He claims that the Doctrine is very much alive and relevant. Conditions in the 1960s are similar to those of the 1820s in that they involve a threat of the extension of "an alien political system" to the New World and the danger of establishment of a "colony" by a European power. It remains only for the heirs of Monroe to apply his principles and issue a similar warning. But the student might well ask whether nineteenth-century standards are always applicable without modification to twentieth-century problems.

So the student of history is frequently confronted with varying interpretations of the same event. This pamphlet is designed to provide training in reading them with critical judgment. The questions posed by the editor in the introduction and headnotes will give the reader some guidance in assessing the selections, and it is hoped that the reader will sharpen his analytical skill by posing his own questions and by challenging the statements and arguments in the selections when they seem inconsistent, illogical, oversimplified, or biased beyond the normal bounds of an author's partiality.

THE ANALYSTS CLASH

The Monroe Doctrine was directed against

the Continental Allies

"The famous declaration of December 2, 1863 . . . had a dual origin and a dual purpose. On the one hand, it was the result of the advance of Russia on the northwest coast of America, and was designed to serve as a protest against this advance and to establish a general principle against Russian expansion. . . . On the other hand, the message was provoked by the fear of European intervention in South America to restore to Spain her revolted colonies, and was intended to give warning of the hostility of the United States to any such intervention."—Dexter Perkins, *The Monroe Doctrine, 1823–1826* (Cambridge, Mass., 1927).

England

"England was the key Power in the formation of American foreign policy . . . and it should be recalled here that even those who advocated joining her in a declaration of policy did so principally because they sought a means of protecting their country from her hostility."—Edward H. Tatum, Jr., *The United States and Europe, 1815–1823* (Berkeley, Calif., 1936).

France

"Further evidence that the Monroe Doctrine was not directed primarily against British designs on Cuba or on Latin America at large is furnished by Monroe's own statement that it was directed primarily against France."—Arthur P. Whitaker, *The United States and the Independence of Latin America, 1800–1830* (Baltimore, 1941).

Ideas embodied in the Doctrine originated with

Adams

"To originate the idea, to carry it in the face of all opposition, to bring Monroe to its support and make him the spokesman—this was distinctly the work of Adams."—Worthington C. Ford, "John Quincy Adams and the Monroe Doctrine" [*American Historical Review*, VIII (1902), 52].

Monroe

"I believe . . . that President Monroe should have the credit not only of announcing this great doctrine, but of being capable, in every sense of the word, of conceiving the act and taking the full responsibility of throwing into the teeth of the world the great principle . . ."—William A. MacCorkle, *The Personal Genesis of the Monroe Doctrine* (New York, 1923).

Jefferson

"Jefferson, then, more than any other individual, was responsible for the basic doctrine of Monroe's message of 1823."—T. R. Schellenberg, "Jeffersonian Origins of the Monroe Doctrine." [*Hispanic American Historical Review,* XIV (1934)].

national policy expressing the thoughts of many

"What is the answer to the much discussed question of the 'authorship' of the Monroe Doctrine? One thing is certain. It was a native national product. No one person was its author. It grew out of a half-century of American independence and republican success. . . . It embodied the experience of American diplomacy. . . . It crystallized the instinctive aversion of American popular sovereignty to European monarchy, colonization, and imperialism."—Samuel Flagg Bemis, *John Quincy Adams and the Foundations of American Foreign Policy* (New York, 1949).

Britain's overtures resulted from

considerations for the balance of power

"Canning's system of policy, indeed . . . was opportunistic and mechanical. The interests of Great Britain were to be regarded as a plane, which if depressed in any part, must be restored to its general level by elevation elsewhere. In carrying out the system, he endeavored by favoring revolution in Spanish America to counter the success of legitimacy in Spain, where the French armies had restored despotic governments. To further the plan he called for the help of the United States."—W. F. Reddaway, *The Monroe Doctrine* (New York, 1905).

the need for markets for growing industry

"And George Canning approached Richard Rush not only as the conscious diplomatist but also as the partly unconscious servant of the energies of British coal and iron, of British spindles and furnaces."—George Dangerfield, *The Era of Good Feelings* (New York, 1952).

The name most closely identified with the historiography of the Monroe Doctrine is DEXTER PERKINS (1889–   ). He began his academic career with a doctoral thesis on the Doctrine which was the first scholarly and comprehensive work on the subject and the first to rely upon manuscript and printed sources from every country connected with the events leading to the Monroe message. Perkins sees the origin of the Doctrine in the international diplomatic situation in the years following the Napoleonic Wars. Does he focus too narrowly on diplomatic events in Europe and ignore public attitudes in the United States?*

To Deter the Continental Allies
in the Western Hemisphere

The famous declaration of December 2, 1823, which has come to be known as the Monroe Doctrine, had a dual origin and a dual purpose. On the one hand, it was the result of the advance of Russia on the northwest coast of America, and was designed to serve as a protest against this advance and to establish a general principle against Russian expansion. Referring to this question of the northwest, President Monroe laid down the principle in his message to Congress that "the American continents, by the free and independent condition which they have assumed and maintain, are henceforth not to be considered as subjects for future colonization by any European powers." On the other hand, the message was provoked by the fear of European intervention in South America to restore to Spain her revolted colonies, and was intended to give warning of the hostility of the United States to any such intervention. "With the governments [that is, of the Spanish-American republics] who have declared their independence, and maintained it," wrote the President, "and whose independence we have, on great consideration and just principles, acknowledged, we could not view any interposition for the purpose of oppressing them, or controlling in any other manner their destiny, by any European power, in any other light than as

* Reprinted by permission of the publishers from Dexter Perkins, *The Monroe Doctrine, 1823–1826,* pp. 3–15, 52–74. Cambridge, Mass:. Harvard University Press. Copyright 1927 by the President and Fellows of Harvard College. Copyright 1955 by Dexter Perkins. Footnotes omitted by permission of the publisher.

the manifestation of an unfriendly disposition toward the United States." . . .

Russian interest in the northwest coast of America goes back to the second quarter of the eighteenth century, to the days of the renowned navigator Vitus Behring, who discovered in 1727 the Straits that now bear his name, and fourteen years later the Alaskan coast in the neighborhood of latitude 58. Behring's explorations were followed by the voyages of fur traders and by the establishment of trading posts on the islands off the American mainland. After years of demoralizing competition on the part of private individuals, the Tsar determined to create a commercial monopoly for the exploitation of the rich fisheries to be found in that part of the world. By the ukase of July 8, 1799, the Russian-American Company was constituted, and to this company were granted exclusive trading rights and jurisdiction along the coast as far south as latitude 55, and the right to make settlements on either side of that line in territory not occupied by other powers. . . .

As time went on . . . the Russian-American Company manifested a distinct tendency toward the extension of its prerogatives. At the end of 1811, or early in 1812, it established a post, named Fort Ross, near Bodega Bay, and not fifty miles from the bay of San Francisco, in a region claimed by Spain. . . . Such a step might easily prove to be the prelude to far-reaching designs of aggrandisement. . . .

It was a later act of overreaching on the part of the Russian-American Company which gave rise to the discussions in the course of which the non-colonization principle was definitely formulated. On September $\frac{4}{16}$,[1] 1821, the Tsar Alexander I, acting at the instigation of the Russian monopoly, promulgated an im-

perial decree which renewed its privileges and confirmed its exclusive trading rights. This time the southern limit of these rights on the American coast was set, not at 55, but at 51 degrees. And in addition, all foreign vessels were forbidden, between Behring Straits and 51 degrees, to come within 100 Italian miles of the shore, on pain of confiscation. A Russian warship was dispatched to the northwest coast to enforce this remarkable decree, and every intention was manifested of barring all other nations from any participation whatever in the trade or fisheries of the region. Such a course of action very naturally provoked a protest, not only on the part of the United States, but also on the part of Great Britain. At this time the two Anglo-Saxon powers had joint ownership, under the convention of 1818, of the territory north from 42 degrees to a line yet to be determined, and the Russian claims of exclusive jurisdiction as far south as 51 degrees could hardly fail to be disquieting. Both from London and from Washington, therefore, came strong diplomatic remonstrance, and thus began a controversy which was to have the closest relationship to the famous pronouncement of 1823. . . .

There is some evidence that, at a date much earlier than 1823, Adams had begun to think of the American continents, especially the North American, as a special preserve of the United States, from which the rest of the world ought to be excluded. The world, he declared in a cabinet meeting of November, 1819, must be

familiarized with the idea of considering our proper dominion to be the continent of

[1] The two dates reflect the Julian and Gregorian calenders. The first number represents the Julian (in use in Russia); the second, the Gregorian (in use in the West).—*Ed.*

North America. From the time when we became an independent people it was as much a law of nature that this should become our pretension as that the Mississippi should flow to the sea. Spain had possessions upon our southern and Great Britain upon our northern border. It was impossible that centuries should elapse without finding them annexed to the United States. . . . Until Europe shall find it a settled geographical element that the United States and North America are identical, any effort on our part to reason the world out of a belief that we are ambitious will have no other effect than to convince them that we add to our ambition hypocrisy.

. . . It is no occasion for surprise, then, to find the secretary by November, 1822, informing the British minister with his usual downrightness that "the whole system of modern colonization was an abuse of government, and it was time that it should come to an end." Here was merely another step toward the assertion of a general theory, a theory which he was finally to formulate in connection with the discussions with the Russian government over the ukase of 1821.

These discussions, begun in 1822, assumed little importance till the late spring of 1823. By that time it had been agreed that the question should be threshed out at St. Petersburg. In June the cabinet discussed the instructions which were to be sent to Mr. Middleton, American minister at the court of the Tsar. The Secretary of State declared it to be his conviction that the United States ought to contest the right of the Russian government to any territorial establishment on the American continents. Apparently this point of view did not pass unchallenged. It was pointed out that Russia would have little reason to accept such drastic doctrine. The United States, in maintaining it, would

be asking everything, and conceding virtually nothing. A compromise was suggested and agreed upon by which this country would recognize the territorial claims of the Tsar north of 55 degrees. On this basis, the negotiations were actually to be conducted.

But Adams, with a curious inconsistency, did not on this account surrender the principle which was taking shape in his mind. At the very moment when he was perfecting the instructions to Middleton along the lines agreed upon in the cabinet, he declared himself to Tuyll, the Russian minister at Washington, in language very much more sweeping.

I told him specially [he writes in his diary, alluding to an interview of July 17, 1823], that we should contest the right of Russia to *any* territorial establishment on this continent, and that we should assume distinctly the principle that the American continents are no longer subjects for *any* new European colonial establishments.

In this statement, almost five months before the appearance of the President's message, we have the non-colonization principle full-fledged, no longer merely a subject of cabinet debate, but explicitly put forward to the minister of the power perhaps most concerned in denying it. . . .

Adams secured Monroe's assent to his new principle in July . . . Whether that assent was cordial and positive, or whether it was given as a mere matter of routine, we have no way of knowing. The President may have warmly approved the non-colonization doctrine; he may, on the other hand, have been little aware of its significance or its implications. On this point his writings provide us with no illumination. But at any rate, he *did* accept it. When, therefore, the Secretary of State drew up in November, the customary sketch of the topics of foreign policy which might interest the President in connection with the preparation of the forthcoming message, he naturally included in the paragraph on the Russian negotiations a reference to the new dogma. That paragraph was taken over almost without verbal change by Monroe, and thus it appeared in his communication to the Congress. These facts are clear, for we have the actual manuscript of Adams's outline of the diplomatic matters which he wished to draw to the attention of the President, and the language of that outline, so far as the non-colonization principle is concerned, corresponds almost exactly with the language of the message itself.

There was, apparently, no consideration of the principle in the cabinet discussion preceding the publication of the President's declaration. On this point Calhoun, then Secretary of War, was to testify many years later, and the silence of Adams's diary at the time confirms this testimony. There is, after all, nothing strange in such a circumstance. For the question of the hour, in November, 1823, was not the dispute with Russia, but the menace offered by the Holy Alliance to the independence of the States of South America. It was on these problems that all the debates turned; so, very naturally, the other problem was crowded out.

Perhaps, however, the fact that Monroe did not call the attention of his official family to the non-colonization dogma may serve to indicate that he did not attach to it the importance which it has since assumed. In all probability, the words which have exercised so great an influence on American thought, on American public opinion, and on American policy, were pronounced, like many

another important declaration, with little realization of the great role which they were to play in the future. Even Adams, with his insight and experience, could hardly have realized how great would be the future of the doctrine which he brought forward in 1823. . . .

The fall of 1822 and the winter of 1823 were to furnish new and striking evidence of the strength of the reaction in the Old World. In October was held the Congress of Verona. At this Congress, the allied powers, not content with the suppression of revolution in Piedmont and Naples, had moved on toward intervention in Spain. In this instance, France, not Austria, was to be the agent of their repressive designs. Great Britain dissenting, it was agreed by the representatives of the great Continental states that they should follow a common policy with respect to Spain, and should morally support the French government if it found it necessary to march its armies into the Peninsula. . . .

In January, after a struggle in the bosom of the cabinet, the French ministry of Villèle virtually determined upon war, and recalled its ambassador from Madrid. In April, the forces of Louis XVIII, under the command of the Duc d'Angoulême, crossed the Pyrenees and began their victorious march on Madrid. The opposition of the revolutionists rapidly crumbled; in a few months the French were in almost complete possession of the country, with the exception of Cadiz, whither the liberal leaders had fled with Ferdinand as their captive. Order had been restored in Europe. Only the New World remained in revolution. Was the next step in the triumphal progress of reaction to be the suppression of the new governments of Spanish America?

Throughout the winter and spring

of 1822–23, the President and Adams seem to have remained tolerably calm as to the danger of any such intervention. Monroe's message of 1822 does, it is true, allude to the course of events in Europe in a tone of foreboding. But he does not speak specifically of the Spanish colonial question, and his words, standing as they do in close relation to an appeal for increased military expenditures, seem to have something of the character of special pleading. They are a slender basis on which to build any theory whatever. The effort to connect them specifically with the Monroe Doctrine seems to be lacking in logic. Nothing else in the correspondence of the President indicates that he was as yet seriously concerned as to the peril in which the new states stood.

Adams, too, even in the spring of 1823, after French interference in Spain had become certain, does not seem to have been disturbed as to the possibility of allied intervention in the New World. What did disturb him, beyond a doubt, was the fate of the island of Cuba. The dispatch of April 28, 1823, in which he set forth to Hugh Nelson, the new American minister to Spain, his views on the subject, has often been quoted in connection with the evolution of the Monroe Doctrine. In reality, it stands a little aside from the main line of events which led up to the President's message. There is only one sentence which alludes to the possibilites of intervention on the South-American continent, and that sentence declares that the purposes of the Continental powers have "not been sufficiently disclosed." Even those portions of the dispatch which refer to Cuba are filled with distrust, not of France and her allies, but of Great Britain. The conquest of the island by France, Adams did not regard as likely, on account of the "probable incompetency of the French maritime force to effect the conquest, and the probability that its accomplishment would be resisted by Great Britain." In case of successful intervention in Spain, there would be, he thought, "no disposition, either in Ferdinand or his allies, to transfer the only remaining colonies of Spain to another power." What he dreaded was that Great Britain would take advantage of the situation to secure the cession of the island, perhaps as the price of her aid to the Spanish constitutionalists against the French. This view he developed at great length and with much force. But there is nothing in the dispatch to Nelson which indicates a growing fear and suspicion of the designs of the Holy Alliance in the New World. . . .

So far, then, as the views of Europe on the colonial question were known in the summer of 1823, they were not a matter of great concern. At the end of August, the American Secretary of State left Washington for a month and a half's visit to his home at Quincy, an almost certain indication that he did not anticipate a diplomatic crisis. There was, as yet, hardly an intimation of the momentous problems that were soon to engage the attention of the administration. The events that were to create an entirely new atmosphere at Washington and produce the Monroe Doctrine are, first, the historic interviews of George Canning with Richard Rush, and, second, two fateful communications from the Tsar. . . .

The increasing friendliness of American sentiment toward Great Britain in the months preceding the interviews between Rush and Canning is not difficult to understand.

With regard to the course of events in Europe, the United States and Great

Britain were on a similar footing. Both held much the same views concerning the new doctrines by which the great Continental powers assumed a right of intervention in the interests of European order. From the first, Great Britain had balked at any such principle, refusing to associate herself with the decisions of Troppau and Laybach,[2] and earning thereby the commendation of the American Secretary of State. Still more, as we have seen, had the British government objected to the French invasion of Spain. And here again, its objections were fully shared by the administration at Washington. Monroe, under the influence of the events of the spring of 1823, began to consider if the time had not come to speak out against the pernicious doctrines of the Old World. In a too little noticed letter to Thomas Jefferson, of June 2, 1823, he wrote as follows: "Our relation to it [the state of Europe] is pretty much the same, as it was, in the commencement of the French revolution. Can we, in any form, take a bolder attitude in regard to it, in favor of liberty, than we then did? Can we afford greater aid to that cause, by assuming any such attitude, than we now do, by the form of our example?" And Adams, despite his natural asperity, found himself admitting to Stratford Canning, the British minister, that England's attitude on the Spanish question was highly gratifying to American opinion, "more particularly as it affected the great principle of national independence, which he seemed to consider as brought into immediate danger by what he termed, the impending conflict, between 'autocracy and parliamentary government.'"

The course which you have taken in the great politics of Europe [wrote Stratford

[2] Congresses held by the "concert of Europe" to discuss measures for maintaining the peace.—*Ed.*

Canning to his cousin in a private letter of May 8, 1823] has had the effect of making the English almost popular in the United States. The improved tone of public feeling is very perceptible, and even Adams has caught a something of the soft infection. The communication of your correspondence with France has also had its effect. On the whole, I question whether for a long time there has been so favorable an opportunity—as far as general disposition and good will are concerned—to bring the two Countries nearer together. France for the moment is quite out of fashion. It may possibly be worth your while to give this a turn in your thoughts.

Stratford Canning's intimation that "even Adams had caught a something of the soft infection" was soon most strikingly borne out by the tone and bearing of the Secretary of State.

Great Britain [he told the British minister] had separated herself from the councils and measures of the alliance. She avowed the principles which were emphatically those of this country, and she disapproved the principles of the alliance, which this country abhorred. The coincidence of principle, connected with the great changes in the affairs of the world, passing before us, seemed to me a suitable occasion for the United States and Great Britain to compare their ideas and purposes together, with a view to the accommodation of great interests upon which they had heretofore differed.

These observations, considering the stiffness of Adams's diplomatic manners, were cordial indeed. They were accompanied by concrete suggestions for an agreement, not only on such questions as the slave trade, and the terms of intercourse with the British-American colonies, but also on such more remote matters as the principles of maritime law and neutral rights. The Secretary furthermore pointed out the identity of views between the two governments on the South American question, and, though he very definitely disavowed any notion of or desire for an alliance, his tone seemed to indicate that he was not unready for a diplomatic rapproachement. By the summer of 1823, therefore, George Canning might logically have assumed than any overtures on his part for common action in the South American question would meet with success. He was not acting without foreknowledge when he made the famous proposals to Richard Rush which had so much to do with the Monroe Doctrine. In view of the change of tone at Washington, what more natural than that he should turn to the United States for support in his South American policy? Were not the circumstances highly favorable to an understanding between the two governments? . . .

The occasion for an exchange of views with regard to French designs on South America was in the first instance furnished, not by Canning, but by the American minister. On August 16, in a conference with the British Foreign Secretary, Rush "transiently asked him" concerning the course of events upon the Continent, and remarked that "should France ultimately effect her purpose of overthrowing the constitutional government in Spain, there was at least the consolation left, that Great Britain would not allow her to go farther and stop the progress of emancipation in the colonies." He also mentioned the British note of March 31,[3] and observed that he considered it as "sufficiently distinct in its import, that England would not remain passive," under any attempt on the part of France to acquire territory in America, "either by conquest or by

[3] In this note to the British minister in Paris, Canning stated that he was "satisfied" that France will not attempt to "bring under her dominion" any part of the "*late* Spanish possessions in America."—*Ed.*

cession from Spain." To these observations, Canning replied with a proposal for a common understanding, asking Rush what he thought his government would say to going hand in hand with England in such a policy. He did not think that concert of action would become necessary, but believed that "the simple fact of our two countries being known to hold the same opinion" would check the French government in any ambitious enterprise it might entertain. "This belief was founded, he said, upon the large share of the maritime power of the world which Great Britain and the United States held, and the consequent influence which the knowledge of their common policy, on a question involving such important maritime interests, present and future, could not fail to produce everywhere."

To these overtures Richard Rush returned a noncommittal reply. He had no intructions on the subject, and to take, without instructions, a step so decisive as that proposed would have been rash indeed. The danger of intervention in the colonies was as yet vague and indefinite; there was no concrete information in the possession of either the British or the American minister to justify precipitate action, action which might imperil the relations of the United States with France, and involve them in "the federative system of Europe." Moreover, and it is immensely to the credit of the American minister that he perceived this fact, the relations of Great Britain and the United States with the colonies did not rest upon an identical footing. The United States had recognized their independence; Great Britain had not. The United States was irrevocably committed; Great Britain, even in case of temporary cooperation with the United States, would still be free to alter her policy, and to bring it into harmony with that of the Continental allies. Common action ought to rest upon a common basis. The American minister, therefore while declining to commit himself, questioned Canning as to "the precise situation in which England stood in relation to those new communities, and especially on the material point of acknowledging their independence." He thus hinted, in the very first exchange of views, at the necessity of recognition of the new republics by Great Britain as indispensable to joint action, a point of view which was later to be expressed with great vigor by his chief at Washington.

On the twentieth, Canning again raised the question of cooperation. He now wrote a note to Rush setting forth the principles of British policy with regard to the colonies, and suggesting the adhesion of the United States to these principles. "England," he wrote, "had no disguise on the subject."

"She conceived the recovery of the colonies by Spain, to be hopeless.

"That the question of their recognition as Independent States, was one of time and of circumstances.

"That England was not disposed, however, to throw any impediment in the way of an arrangement between the colonies and the mother country, by amicable negotiation.

"That she aimed at the possession of no portion of the colonies for herself.

"That she could not see the transfer of any portion of them to any other Power, with indifference."

Holding these views, Great Britain would be very ready to declare them in concert with the United States. Could Rush sign a convention on the subject? Or, if this were not possible, could he consent to an exchange of ministerial notes? "Nothing could be more gratifying

to me than to join with you in such a work," wrote Canning, "and, I am persuaded, there has seldom, in the history of the world, occurred an opportunity when so small an effort of two friendly Governments might produce so unequivocal a good and prevent such extensive calamities."

Three days after making this overture the British Foreign Secretary received further information, which led him to press even more eagerly for an understanding with the American government. The French Foreign Minister, Chateaubriand, informed Sir Charles Stuart, British ambassador at Paris, that on the termination of the war in Spain a congress would probably be called to deal with the colonial question. This information, speedily transmitted to Canning at Liverpool, led him to write Rush again on August 23, apprising him of the posture of affairs, and urging that the proposal of a congress formed

an additional motive for wishing that we might be able to come to some understanding on the part of our respective Governments on the subject of my letter; to come to it soon, and to be at liberty to announce it to the world. . . . I need not point out to you [he added] all the complications to which this proposal, however dealt with by us, may lead.

Rush replied to these communications of Canning's with an interesting exposition of the general point of view of the United States. In a note of August 23, he emphasized the anxiety of the American government to see the colonies "received into the family of nations by the powers of Europe, and especially by Great Britain." He stated his entire concurrence in the principles laid down in the note of August 20, barring the matter of recognition on which the United States had already made its decision. In a note of the twenty-sixth he indicated that his country "desired to see the Independence of the late Spanish Provinces in America permanently maintained," and that it "would view as unjust and improper any attempt on the part of the Powers of Europe to intrench upon that Independence." He added that the United States "would regard as alike objectionable any interference whatever in the affairs of Spanish America, unsolicited by the late Provinces themselves, and against their will; that it would regard the convening of a Congress to deliberate upon their affairs, as a measure uncalled for, and indicative of a policy highly unfriendly to the tranquillity of the world; that it could never look with insensibility upon such an exercise of European jurisdiction over communities now of right exempt from it, and entitled to regulate their own concerns unmolested from abroad." With regard to the possibility of cooperation the American minister went further than in his previous communication. Indeed, he intimated the possibility of accepting Canning's offer. . . . [He] broadly hinted at the possibility of Anglo-American cooperation if Great Britain would recognize the new republics of South America.

The British Foreign Secretary was not ready, however, for cooperation on such terms. . . . On August 31 he wrote Rush that, pending more definite information on the American viewpoint, he did not wish to tie the hands of Great Britain, and went on to request him to treat his previous communication "*not* as a proposition already made, but as evidence of the nature of one which it would have been his desire to make, had he found me provided with authority to entertain it."

There was, however, a temporary suspension rather than a cessation of the exchange of views between Canning and the American minister. In September, at the request of the former, new conversations took place, and once again joint action was urged by the British Foreign Secretary. . . .

At any rate, the fact that Canning was desirous of cooperating with the United States in the matter of Spanish America was clearly understood in Washington early in October, with the receipt of the dispatches from the American minister in London. For the first time, grave suspicions began to be felt by President Monroe as to the motives and purposes of the Continental powers in the New World. A definite purpose on the part of the allies to reconquer Spanish America had not been alleged by the British Foreign Secretary. But there had been allusions to a congress to discuss the colonial problem, and Rush himself had been led to believe that serious dangers were impending. In the face of such facts, it was necessary seriously to consider what should be the attitude of the United States.

The news of the British overtures, therefore, stimulated an earnest discussion of the colonial question at Washington. In the course of the next two months, after the most careful consideration, Monroe and Adams were to prepare and launch a warning to Europe against interference across seas, and to challenge the reigning doctrines by which the sovereigns of the Old World affected to be guided. . . .

The arrival at Washington of the news of Canning's first interviews with Rush was speedily followed by other events of high importance. On October 16, Baron Tuyll called on the Secretary of State and informed him that the Tsar Alexander would not receive any minister or agent from any one of the states just formed in the New World. He also expressed the satisfaction of the Russian government at the attitude of neutrality that had been observed by the United States in the colonial conflict, and at its declared intention to continue to maintain that neutrality.

The views thus more or less informally expressed were embodied in an official note that was transmitted on the same day.

His Imperial Majesty [it stated] . . . faithful to the political principles which he follows in concert with his Allies, cannot under any circumstances receive any agent whatsoever, either from the Regency of Colombia, or from any of the other governments, which owe their existence to the events of which the New World has been for some years the stage.

This declaration of policy on the part of Alexander had been entirely unsolicited by the United States. It came at a time when its exact purpose was extremely difficult to fathom. It was like lightning from a clear sky. True, there was nothing necessarily sinister about it. On its face it was no more than a declaration of the Russian viewpoint on South America, and a commendation of the neutral attitude of the United States. But did it indicate a reviving interest on the part of the Tsar in the colonial question? Why compliment the United States on its neutrality? What political principles were those to which the note alluded? Was there here a veiled reference to the right of intervention in behalf of legitimacy? So the President, at any rate, may have feared, for he directed Adams to seek an explanation of the phrase from Tuyll.

A month later came a communication even more disturbing. It was a note written by Nesselrode,[4] dated August 30,

[4] Russian minister of foreign affairs.

1823, and dealing with the recent intervention in Spain. It was framed, Adams sets down in his diary, in "a tone of passionate exultation," and was

an *"Io Triumphe"* over the fallen cause of revolution, with sturdy promises of determination to keep it down; disclaimers of all intention of making conquests; bitter complaints of being calumniated, and one paragraph of compunctions, acknowledging that an apology is yet due to mankind for the invasion of Spain, which it is in the power only of Ferdinand to furnish, by making his people happy.

There was nothing in this state paper which directly menaced the liberties of the New World, as a careful reading of its full text will serve to show. The Tsar Alexander, indeed, may well have regarded it as a reassuring explanation of the benevolent intentions of the allied powers. In the main, it was a homily on purely Continental affairs, and contained hardly a reference to the New World. The only phrase which could even by the closest construction be taken to hint at a purpose to intervene in the Spanish colonies is that in which the Tsar speaks of a policy, "whose only object is to guarantee the tranquillity of all the states of which the civilized world is composed." But to anyone aware of Alexander's penchant for sonorous phrase, and sweeping generalization, such a sentence was hardly to be taken too seriously. And yet the principles which the note professed, and the tone in which they set forth, could hardly fail to be disturbing to the government at Washington, and to furnish an additional reason for setting forth, without delay and in the most explicit terms, the opposition of the United States to the doctrine of intervention, and to interference by the European powers with the affairs of the New World.

Before Tuyll had presented this dispatch to Adams, however, Monroe and his advisers discussed the dangers in which the Spanish colonies stood. From the beginning of the cabinet discussions of November, 1823, the President and John C. Calhoun, the Secretary of War, were wholly convinced that the Holy Alliance would soon act to restore the colonies to Spain. The President, wrote Adams, "is alarmed far beyond anything that I could have conceived possible," and "the news that Cadiz has surrendered to the French has so affected him that he appeared entirely to despair of the cause of South America." Calhoun, in Adams's phrase, was "perfectly moonstruck" at the danger.

The Secretary of State himself refused to be thus terrified. It is, indeed, not the least striking evidence of his ability as a diplomat that he viewed the situation without panic, and with superb sense of proportion. Five years before, at the time of the deliberations at Aix-La-Chapelle, he had pointed out that the allies had no interest whatsoever in the reconquest of the colonies. This was still his viewpoint in 1823. He believed that the Holy Alliance "would not ultimately invade South America." If they should actually do so, "they might make a temporary impression for three, four, or five years," said Adams in the cabinet meeting of November 15, but "I no more believe that the Holy Allies will restore the Spanish dominion upon the American continent than that the Chimborazo will sink beneath the ocean." They would have no conceivable reason to restore the old exclusive system of the past. Spain could never maintain herself in the New World alone, and "was it in human absurdity to imagine that they [the allied powers] should waste their blood and

treasure to prohibit their own subjects upon pain of death to set foot upon those territories?" If they took action at all, the ultimate result would be to partition the colonies among themselves. But was it reasonable to suppose that they could agree upon any principle or partition? And even if they were able to do so, what inducement could they offer to Great Britain to acquiesce in any such scheme? "The only possible bait they could offer . . . was Cuba, which neither they nor Spain would consent to give her."

But though Adams was very far indeed from the panic fear that the Holy Alliance would reconquer South America, and was strongly inclined to the opinion that no intervention would even be attempted, he was by no means inclined to let the situation pass without an expression of the views of the United States. He believed that the situation required a very definite assertion of American policy. And so, for the matter of that, did all the other members of the cabinet and the President himself. There was not even a disposition to delay action until Canning's overtures could be accepted, and a concert of action established with Great Britain. When Adams, in one of the first of the cabinet meetings, that of November 7, declared that "it would be more candid as well as more dignified, to avow our principles explicitly to Russia and France, than to come in as a cockboat in the wake of the British man-of-war," his idea "was acquiesced in on all sides." President Monroe himself, who leaned toward the acceptance of the British proposals, was heartily averse to taking any attitude that might be regarded as "subordinate," and was ready to make the position of the United States entirely clear.

Whereas Perkins concentrates on the reactions of American political leaders to the diplomatic moves of the European powers, EDWARD H. TATUM, JR. (1908–   ) focuses on the hostility toward England by the American public and on the suspicion of British motives by the Administration. For him, the Monroe Doctrine was a response to Britain's efforts to extend its influence to the New World and the purpose of the Doctrine was to thwart these efforts. To be sure, American fear of interventions by European powers played a part in precipitating the statement but the more important factor was the impression conveyed to President Monroe that English policy constituted the real danger to the United States. Does Tatum overrate Anglo-American hostility?*

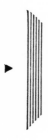

To Forestall Britain's Designs on Cuba and New World Markets

The Monroe Doctrine had its immediate origin in the events of the fall of 1823, but it cannot be divorced from the experiences of the preceding years. It would be very easy to explain the President's message by emphasizing the superficial aspects of the problem, but that would not result in an accurate interpretation. The Monroe Doctrine was the result of forces which had been at work in the United States for years, forces whose influence was becoming evident even before 1820. The developments of the fall of 1823 brought matters to a crisis, revealed the operation of these underlying elements, and made certain a declaration of policy in that year, but they did not "cause" that result. They formed the "incident" which determined the time of the declaration. The important thing to be remembered is that, by June, 1823, the trend of American thought and experience had been so definitely in the direction of an independent, national, republican foreign policy that a formal statement of it was inevitable. Sooner or later, it would have been made. All that was necessary was a provocative "incident."

Let us recall briefly what may be termed the conditioning factors behind the Monroe Doctrine. The unsettled state

* From Edward H. Tatum, Jr., *The United States and Europe, 1815–1823*, pp. 251–278. Reprinted by permission of the publisher, the University of California Press. Copyright 1936 by the Regents of the University of California. Footnotes omitted by permission of the publisher.

of Europe, which Monroe likened to that of 1789, was a constant source of concern to Americans. The Continent appeared to be upon the threshold of a new era of internal revolution and international war. There never had been a time in the history of America when war in Europe had not affected the lives of the people in the western hemisphere. Although Americans did not know how they would become implicated in this new strife, they were haunted by the fear that the old series of developments would be repeated. War in Europe would sooner or later involve England, and, once she entered the fray, the interests of the United States would be threatened. Therefore, the spectacle of Europe at war aroused apprehensions. While America's relations with France and Russia were reasonably satisfactory and while there was no reason to suspect those Powers of hostile designs, problems were pending which required careful diplomacy for their solution. Only by maintaining an attitude of aloofness and impartiality could the United States hope to succeed. Relations with England were much less promising, and her sea power made her a dangerous adversary.

The temper of the public influenced the government at every turn. The steady progress of resentment against England *per se* reached a climax in 1822–1823, and a distinct anti-English bias in the national thought resulted. The course of English policy had increased this tendency. Recent occurrences in Europe had reanimated popular antagonism against Old World principles and reactionary government.[1] American nationalism was of a very emotional type during this period and was easily stirred. The actions of the Powers at Verona and of France in Spain evoked expressions of pride in

American institutions and of sympathy for the oppressed peoples of Europe. From this state of mind resulted much inconsistency and uncertainty of purpose. Americans became enthusiastic at the idea of aiding the Greeks to recover their former glories and at the same time demanded increased appropriations for defense against the possible attacks of foreign enemies. This confusion of judgment was increasing in 1823, and the need for directing Americans along the paths of reasonableness was becoming apparent.

Yet another conditioning element is to be found in the fact that, while the United States had declared its policy plainly to France and to Russia, the state of its relations with England made it very difficult to come to any understanding with that Power. England could not be threatened, since America had not the bargaining power which enabled her to be outspoken with France and Russia. *They* did not want to drive the United States into the arms of England, and knowledge of this desire gave the United States considerable influence. But was it possible to convince England that American opposition to her expansion in Oregon or in the areas to the south of the United States would injure English interests? A direct threat might only make matters worse yet the United States would never be secure so long as there was the possibility of the extension of English political influence in the western hemisphere. The equivocal position of England in world affairs at this time

[1] In previous chapters, Tatum describes the antipathy of the American people to the repressive measures of the Quadruple Alliance and the increased antagonism toward England caused by suspicion of English commercial and territorial ambitions in the Western Hemisphere.—*Ed.*

made the need for blocking her power more and more pressing.

The growing preoccupation of the people of the United States with internal affairs also had an influence upon her foreign relations. Westward expansion, the effects of a growing national spirit upon sectional interests, and the complex problems which the Industrial Revolution had produced were directing American development into new channels. The feeling that the United States and the New World were so different from Europe and England that nothing was to be gained from close contact with them was increased by the orientation of internal affairs. In addition, these new problems limited the freedom of action of the United States. Previously, the solution for pressing problems in the areas near the borders had been the seizure or purchase of territory. In this fashion the Louisiana and Florida questions had been settled. But sectional differences, which the admission of Missouri had revealed, precluded the further use of these means. The United States found itself in the very difficult position of a relatively weak nation attempting to maintain the *status quo* in the collapsing colonial empire of another weak Power then engaged in war. Such a situation would have taxed the diplomatic ability of any government. It is indeed a tribute to the diplomacy of the critical decade of the twenties that the interests of the country were protected as well as they were during the nineteenth century.

The unsettled state of European politics, the attitude of the public toward the foreign situation, fear of the power of England, and internal conditions combined to direct the thoughts of American diplomats toward a clear definition of their policy, but certain developments in

the fall of 1823 made an immediate declaration a necessity. These determining factors, as they may be called, were three in number. For the first time, the American press began to hint that the peace and happiness of the United States were at stake as a result of the crusade of the French into Spain. Early in 1823, the general view was that there was "nothing to fear" from the aims of the European autocrats. During the summer, however, a change was noticeable. The so-called treaty of Verona[2] was published in *Niles' Weekly Register* in August; and in September Niles[3] predicted that "we shall have no small difficulties with the powers of Europe" and that probably American rights would not be respected by the reactionary rulers.

Earlier in the year, *The Edinburgh Review* had published an article which condemned the Holy Alliance and demanded that the English government intervene on behalf of Spain in order to prevent an attack upon its own institutions! This partisan dissertation found an echo in the article which appeared in October in *The North American Review*. Interpreting the same collection of documents which had called forth the remarks of its Scottish contemporary, the Boston journal allowed its fancy free rein. It declared that the Holy Alliance planned the destruction of the English constitution and would achieve that end by the same means that had been employed in Naples and in Spain! Assuming, quite logically from this startling premise, that no free nation on earth

---

[2] The treaty signed at the Congress of Verona (1822). France was authorized by the European allies to invade Spain for the purpose of restoring the dethroned Ferdinand VII.—*Ed.*

[3] Hezekiah Niles was editor of the important weekly journal that bore his name. Published in Baltimore, it had a national circulation and was influential in molding public opinion.—*Ed.*

was safe, the *Review* asked: "Would not the Spanish colonies, as part of the same empire, then demand their parental attention? And might not the United States be next considered as deserving their kind guardianship?" Why not, indeed? The article further expressed the suspicion that Russia had plans for encroaching on American rights on the Northwest Coast as part of a systematic policy directed against the United States. Significantly enough, even in its wildest flights the *Review* did not lose sight of the threat of English action.

. . . If England should join Spain in her conquest with France, the chance of this country's remaining at peace will be still more diminished. Great Britain is a greater monopolist of the commerce of the world than even Spain. Her commercial system has extended itself into every quarter, and has been everywhere followed and supported by her wealth, her intrigues, and her arms. In America, Europe, Asia, and Africa, it is seen and felt, grasping and monopolizing the commerce and carrying trade of all nations. Every war has its preservation for an object, and every negotiation tends to extend and perpetuate it. . . .

Just as Calhoun and Jackson exaggerated the power of the Holy Alliance but feared equally the threat of English intervention, so *The North American Review* fell into the same line of thought and, similarly, concluded with an appeal for increased measures of national defense.

These articles happened to coincide with the arrival in America of the news of the fall of Cadiz, with the result that in November a slight panic occurred in some quarters. Calhoun was not the only person who became "moonstruck" at the prospect of French power, and, though there was almost no foundation for the

Review's statements, they influenced the public. Niles asked his readers the same rhetorical questions which the Boston periodical had proposed, and even the *National Intelligencer* admitted that "The day may come, sooner than we have thought on, when these ['our fortified coast and our gallant navy'] may not only be *our* defence, but a barrier to preserve the remaining liberties of the world." With sounder insight than Niles, however, the organ of the administration declared that the pent-up volcano in Europe would soon explode with greater fierceness than before.

While the problem of possible interference with the affairs of the New World is being considered, one or two collateral developments may be mentioned. There is no doubt that in October and November there was current in the United States a sense of apprehension of French power, but it is also plain that it was not a deep-seated conviction, but rather a momentary manifestation caused by a few alarmist articles and by the fall of Cadiz. It is also interesting to observe that both Niles and *The North American Review* were strong supporters of the Greek cause and that both argued for active interference in European affairs at the time when they were voicing fears of attacks upon the very existence of the United States. The *Review* had sounded "the clarion call of American Philhellenism" in the same issue which contained the article on the Holy Alliance. Such confusion of thought and judgment was a general phenomenon and throws a great deal of light upon the public spirit. Those who were most inclined to fear attacks upon the United States clamored most loudly for the United States to interfere actively in European affairs by aiding the Greek patriots.

The administration took a saner, more reasoned attitude toward the whole matter and adopted a consistent course. It is significant that when these apprehensions were being aired, one paper steadfastly reiterated its disbelief in them. The editor of *The Enquirer* "repeatedly assured his countrymen that they had nothing to fear from the tyrants of Europe." Thomas Ritchie[4] was very intimate with the Virginia statesmen and was informed of the progress of diplomatic developments. His conclusions therefore reveal the state of mind of the members of the government. As his biographer rightly notes, "his predictions regarding the intentions of the continental Powers in America must have had a better foundation than the belief that Great Britain would not aid them." In spite of the opinions of *The Enquirer* there was a rather general feeling in the country that all was not well with its foreign relations. This, too, was a matter which required the attention of the government.

While the state of public opinion was thus one of the determining factors, the suggestion which George Canning made to Rush for a joint declaration of policy was a second and even more important one. This English overture further unsettled and complicated the problems of the United States. It raised vague anxieties for the unknown future and misgivings about the real nature of English policy. It forced the United States to act and to act immediately. Canning's proposal could either be accepted or rejected. If it were rejected America would have to make a separate declaration. This implication of a refusal to join England is often overlooked. If England were not bound by her own promises, it was abso-

4 Editor of *The Enquirer—Ed.*

lutely imperative that the policy of the United States should be placed in a clear light, so that there could be no possible misunderstanding of its character. Canning's action, therefore, was decisive for the United States.

The third factor which made a declaration of American policy certain was the Russian minister's communications to Adams in October and November. These impersonal statements of the essential soundness of monarchical principles and the resolution of the Tsar not to recognize the South American republics were received when there was little chance of their being disregarded by the administration. They were not threats, and none of the members of the government so regarded them. The spirit of the country, however, made a reply, a counterstatement, natural and indispensable. Above all, the Russian notes afforded a magnificent opportunity to make the statement general. It could be an answer to Russia as well as to England, and it could be couched in terms which would include the Old World as a whole.

These three developments, added to the more general forces already discussed, made necessary the declaration of policy which Monroe included in his message to Congress. It is not surprising, therefore, that the reaction of the administration and its advisers to the events of October and November reflected quite accurately the currents of thought which had so long been gathering force. It is unnecessary to narrate again the details of the correspondence between Canning and Rush and the reports of the American minister to the secretary of state. If the phases of English policy are sketched briefly and the reaction of American statesmen to those developments is emphasized, the connection between the history of the postwar years and the Monroe Doctrine will be established, and a truer understanding of that policy will be obtained.

In August, 1823, Rush had expressed to Canning his understanding that it was the policy of England to prevent any interference by France in the New World. To his surprise, the foreign secretary replied by suggesting an Anglo-American declaration to that effect. No mention was made of any immediate danger of French action, nor was it even affirmed that France had any intention of interfering in the New World. At the same time, moreover, Canning refused to state definitely that the colonies were irrevocably lost to Spain. A few days after this interview, he wrote the communication to Rush in which he outlined the form of the proposed declaration. Again he did not say positively that any European Power had plans for the reduction of the revolted colonies. However, Rush's steadfast refusal to act in concert apparently led Canning to intimate that a congress was planned for the near future. But this report was suspiciously indefinite.

I have received notice . . . [he wrote] that so soon as the military objects in Spain are achieved . . . a proposal will be made for a Congress, or some less formal concert and consultation, specially upon the affairs of Spanish America.

Even Rush realized that this information did not impose the necessity of instant action and adhered firmly to his demand for English recognition of South American independence *first* and for a joint declaration second.

The information revealed by the interview of August 16 and by the letters of August 20 and 23[5] was sent to Washington by Rush with explanations of his stand. These dispatches were received on October 9 and formed the basis of the first steps taken by Monroe. The President felt that the time had arrived when England must make a decision between despotism and liberty and that she had adopted this means of announcing her choice. He assumed that this was an occasion on which a European connection might safely be made by the United States and was inclined to believe that an attack on the colonies would be followed by a move against the United States. These impressions were recorded in the letter of October 17 in which Monroe asked Jefferson and Madison for their advice on the subject.

Madison's reply was cautious. He regarded Canning's move as a confirmation of the current idea that a "crusade" against South America was planned. He approved the project for a joint declaration and thought it "particularly fortunate" that England was ready to cooperate, for with her support "we have nothing to fear from the rest of Europe." But Madison, admittedly uninformed on the details of foreign relations, misunderstood the extent of England's conversion to liberal principles when he suggested that she might be induced to condemn the invasion of Spain by France and to declare her support of the Greeks. Although his thought was confused about the consistency of such action, it is clear that he regarded England as the key to the future and that he esteemed the chance to draw her over to the side of free government as worth the abandonment of America's policy of independent action. Significantly, he raised the ques-

[5] The substance of the conversation and the notes is in the Perkins selection, pp. 17–18.—*Ed.*

tion of the effect which an acceptance of Canning's proposal would have on the future of Cuba and Porto Rico. His views were rather vague and general, however, and he asked as many questions as he answered.

Jefferson was better informed upon the subject of world politics than was Madison, and his reply to Monroe gained definiteness as a result. In a letter which has rightly become a classic of American political literature, Jefferson formulated the principles on which the foreign policy of the United States should be based: the noninterference of America in European affairs, and the prevention of European intervention in the affairs of the New World. At the outset, Jefferson avoided the confusion of thought which misled every member of the administration except John Quincy Adams. If America desired to maintain the *status quo* in the western world, consistency demanded that she take no part in attempts to upset the existing order in Europe.

It is of the greatest interest to notice what Jefferson regarded as the advantage and the disadvantage of an acceptance of Canning's plan. The chief benefit would *not* be the opportunity to block the Holy Alliance, but the chance to limit the danger of *English* hostility.

. . . One nation, most of all [he wrote], could disturb us in this pursuit [of freedom]; she now offers to lead, aid, and accompany us in it. By acceding to her proposition, we detach her from the bands, bring her mighty weight into the scale of free government, and emancipate a continent at one stroke, which might otherwise linger long in doubt and difficulty. Great Britain is the nation which can do us the most harm of anyone, or all on earth; and with her on our side we need not fear the whole world. With her then, we should most sedulously cherish a

cordial friendship; and nothing would tend more to knit our affections than to be fighting once more, side by side, in the same cause. . . . And if, to facilitate this, we can effect a division in the body of the European powers, and draw over to our side its most powerful member, surely we should do it. . . . With Great Britain withdrawn from their scale and shifted into that of our two continents, all Europe combined would not undertake such a war. For how would they propose to get at either enemy without superior fleets? Nor is the occasion to be slighted which this proposition offers, of declaring our protest against the atrocious violations of the rights of nations, by the interference of any one in the affairs of another, so flagitiously begun by Bonaparte, and now continued by the equally lawless Alliance, calling itself Holy.

This clear recognition of England's sea power and the value to the United States of removing it as a threat is of the greatest importance, for it reveals the way in which a very influential and very experienced American interpreted the foreign scene. *Only* in the event of a combination of England with the European Powers would the New World be seriously endangered.

The disadvantage of participating in a declaration of the sort suggested by Canning lay in the fact that that would prevent the United States from acquiring Cuba. But even the sacrifice of this valuable island was of secondary significance. The greatest danger which confronted the United States, the occupation of Cuba by England, would be averted.

Yet, as I am sensible that this can never be obtained [American possession of Cuba], even with her own consent, but by war; and its independence, which is our second interest, (and especially its independence of England,) can be secured without it, I have no hesitation in abandoning my first wish to future chances, and accepting its independence, with peace and the friendship of England, rather than its association, at the expense of war and her enmity.

To tie the hands of England in the New World was worth the abandonment of Cuba, the surrender of the principle of independent action, and the limitation of freedom to expand southward and westward. This was a high price; that Jefferson was willing to pay it is proof of his respect for the power of England in world affairs.

Hardly had Monroe received the replies of Jefferson and Madison when additional dispatches arrived from Rush which completely changed the earlier aspect of the negotiation. Canning had refused to recognize South America,[6] Rush reported, and had also declined to wait until the American minister could receive instructions from his government. The foreign secretary had therefore asked Rush to forget the whole affair and to consider the proposal nonexistent. In a letter to the secretary of state, Rush related in detail the arguments which Canning had used to induce him to act immediately. The tone of the dispatch makes it clear that Rush suspected ulterior motives for the haste displayed by Canning. This distrust was further revealed in a private letter to Monroe which reached Washington on November 3 with the second set of dispatches. Rush was in the habit of writing private notes to his friend, and there is no doubt that they influenced the President. All the ingrained suspicion of England so characteristic of American thought is here.

I am bound to own that I shall not be able to avoid, at bottom, some distrust of the

[6] Tatum means, of course, the former Spanish colonies in South America.—*Ed.*

motives of all such advances to me, whether directly or indirectly, by this government, at this particular juncture of the world.

We have seen her wage a war of 20 years at a cost of treasure and blood incalculable, in support of the independence of other states (as she said) when that independence was threatened by a movement proceeding from the *people* of France. We have seen her at the close of that contest abandoning the great interests of the people of other states, anxious apparently only about monarchs and thrones. We have seen her at the same epoch become in effect a member of the Holy Alliance; though she could not in form, and continue to abet its principles up to the attack on Naples. Even then the separation was but partial, and, true to her sympathy with the monarchical principle, we find her faith pledged and her fleets ready to interpose not on any new extremity of wrong or oppression to the *people* of Naples, but on any molestation to the royal family. . . .

The estimate which I have formed of the genius of this government, as well as of the characters of the men who direct, or who influence, all its operations, would lead me to fear that we are not as yet likely to witness any very material changes in the part which Britain has acted in the world for the past fifty years, when the cause of freedom has been at stake; the part which she acted in 1774 in America, which she has since acted in Europe, and is now acting in Ireland. I shall therefore find it hard to keep from my mind the suspicion that the approaches of her ministers to me at this portentous juncture for a concert of policy which they have not heretofore courted with the United States, are bottomed on their own calculations. I wish that I could sincerely see in them a true concern for the rights and liberties of mankind. Nevertheless, whatever may be the *motive* of these approaches, if they give promise of leading to good *effects* . . . [I shall listen to them].

Despite the last sentence, this letter presents no encouraging picture of English policy. If five years' experience at the English court led Rush to express such sentiments in private correspondence with the President, one may be sure that the general opinion in America was equally skeptical. The way in which Canning dropped the negotiation rankled in the heart of the American minister and made him unusually watchful. He was an admirer of England, as his memoirs indicate, but he had no confidence in the honesty of English policy. In a dispatch to Adams, which was received in the United States on November 19 and which completed the information in the hands of the government, Rush repeated his indictment of England in even stronger terms.

. . . That the British cabinet, and the governing portion of the British nation, will repoice at heart in the downfal of the constitutional system in Spain, I have never had a doubt and have not now, so long as this catastrophe can be kept from crossing the path of British interests and British ambition. This nation in its collective, corporate, capacity has no more sympathy with popular rights and freedom now, than it had on the plains of Lexington in America. . . . With a king in the hands of his ministers, with an aristocracy of unbounded opulence and pride, with what is called a house of commons constituted essentially by this aristocracy and always moved by its influence, England can, in reality, never look with complacency upon popular and equal rights, whether abroad or at home. She therefore moves in her natural orbit when she wars, positively or negatively, against them. For their own sakes alone, she will never war in their favor.

Rush questioned English policy in principle and also felt that concrete reasons for alarm existed. In this same dispatch he told Adams that Canning had informed him that English com-missioners (one of whom had ministerial credentials) had been sent to Mexico and that the English government expected that closer relations between the two countries would result. This move, together with others which Canning revealed, made the future dark indeed. The picture of English policy which Rush gave to Adams is best painted in his own words.

It may perhaps afford room for conjecture what had led to the preference of Mexico over the other ex-colonies for such a provisionary diplomatic representation. I have heard a rumour, that an eye to some immediate advantage from the mines of that country has been the motive. . . . Mr. Canning himself in one of our conversations thought fit to select Mexico as affording a prominent illustration of interior disquiet. Whether then the above rumour is the key to this early preference, or the proximity of this new state to the territories of the United States—or what considerations may have led to it, a little more time will probably disclose. It may rest on the mere fact of her greater population and riches.

Mr. Canning also informed me, that orders would be given by this government to its squadron in the West Indies, to protect the trade of British subjects (to the extent of making reprisals if necessary) with the Spanish colonies, in case the licence for this trade which the Cortes granted in January last was not renewed. It will be recollected, that the same decree of the Cortes in that month which settled, under a threat of reprisals, the British claims upon Spain for captures, laid open the trade of the ultra marine provinces to Britain for ten years. . . .

. . . It will next be seen that her ex-colonies come in for their share of this prompt and summary species of remedy of which Britain is setting other nations the example, for Mr. Canning also informed me that if the Colombian government did not make speedy reparation for the alleged aggression committed upon a British ship by the fort at Bocachica at the entrance of the bay of Carthagena, orders would be given to blockade that port. . . . From the account I have had of it from the Colombian minister in this city, Mr. Ravenga, I infer and believe that the offence was on the side of the British ship.

This was definite information from the foreign secretary himself. No rumors were these, but statements of fact. England had sent agents to Mexico to work for closer relations; she had announced her determination to maintain her privileged position in the trade with Cuba and Porto Rico by reprisals (a euphemistic term for undeclared war); and she had avowed the purpose of coercing one of the independent republics by means of a blockade. England had long been suspected of designs on Mexico, and she had long been charged with seeking to dominate the economic life of Spanish America. Here was proof of her plans, of the actual steps which she had taken toward their execution, and of her supreme indifference to the views of the United States. Canning's very boldness in informing the American minister was disquieting, for the imagination of Americans might wander at will over the possibilities of what had *not* been disclosed. What Power was it, then, that was about to interfere in the New World in 1823? Was it France, who had given every indication that she did not wish to antagonize the United States, who was then engaged in a European war, and concerning whose "plans" only the vaguest rumors in the press and the hints of an *English* diplomat had reached America? Or was it England, who had never once satisfactorily assured the United States of her friendly spirit, who had pursued a uniformly hostile course, and who now

added to a suspicious proposal for joint action the announcement that she contemplated armed interference in the Spanish colonial trade and the actual blockade of the port of an independent South American republic?

It was a foregone conclusion that the cabinet would decline to act with England when it became clear that her proposals lacked sincerity. Adams regarded Canning's moves as attempts to trap the United States into a renunciation of Cuba, and the secretary opposed the making of any such self-denying statement. The future of the United States should be unhampered by inconvenient declarations. The refusal of England to recognize the republics of the south and her reluctance to break completely with the Continental Powers made joint action impossible. Instructions to Rush on November 30 made this view of the American government plain.

. . . Great Britain negotiating at once with the European Alliance, and *with us,* concerning America, without being bound by any permanent community of principle . . . would still be free to accommodate her policy to any of those distributions of power, and partitions of Territory which have for the last half century been the ultima ratio of all European political arrangements. . . .

That sentence is an interesting echo of the past experience of the secretary of state, for he was convinced years before that the early failure of the administration's South American policy had resulted in part from Monroe's willingness to confide in England and to act with her, rather than independently.

The effect of a joint declaration on world politics did not escape the keen eyes of the members of the administration. To range the United States with England would antagonize France and

Russia and would deprive American diplomacy of one of its strongest weapons in the important negotiations which were then being conducted with those Powers. England was a dangerous friend, and the "threat" of Continental action was not real enough to induce the Americans to accept the unpleasant aspects of an *entente* with her.

. . . By taking the step here [wrote Monroe to Jefferson early in December], it is done in a manner more conciliatory with, & respectful to Russia, & the other powers, than if taken in England, and as it is thought with more credit to our govt. Had we mov'd in the first instance in England, separated as she is in part, from those powers, our union with her, being marked, might have produced irritation with them. We know that Russia, dreads a connection between the UStates & G. Britain, or harmony in policy. Moving on our own ground, the apprehension that unless she retreats, that effect may be produced, may be a motive with her for retreating. Had we mov'd in England, it is probable, that it would have been inferr'd that we acted under her influence, & at her instigation, & thus have lost credit as well with our southern neighbours, as with the allied powers.

This is the best commentary on the background of the Monroe Doctrine that has ever been written, for its implications touch the foundations of that policy. Monroe's failure to mention France, his able discussion of the effect of the Balance of Power on American diplomacy, his assumption that the Continental Powers would not force any issue with the United States, and his concluding phrase, "& thus have lost credit as well with our southern neighbours, as with the allied powers," are of the utmost significance. For these very excellent reasons, the administration determined to act alone. All the factors which prompted this decision are related to the central idea that England was not sincere in her offer and that too close a connection with her would injure the foreign relations of the United States.

Coincident with these developments were two communications from Tuyll to Adams. They were circular letters which the Tsar had sent to all his diplomats and they expressed the views of monarchy and of Russian policy which were mentioned above. That Adams should demand the opportunity to answer these declarations of Old World principles with an equally plain statement of the foundations of American institutions is obvious. To him, a proud, clear, and bold utterance of her ideals was a sacred obligation which could not be avoided without dishonor. Neither he nor Monroe regarded the Russian notes as threats to the United States, and both welcomed the opportunity to reply. All the nationalism which had been growing in intensity during the preceding years found expression in the paragraphs of the message which dealt with American principles.

The cabinet discussions which resulted in the Monroe Doctrine have often been analyzed by those who desired to ascertain the authorship of its provisions. As a foreign policy, it is immaterial whether Monroe or Adams enunciated it, for it was a *national* policy decided upon after the fullest consideration by the leaders of the government. What *is* significant about these cabinet meetings is that the views of the active members, Adams, Calhoun, and Monroe, reflected all the conflicting currents of thought which filled the minds of their countrymen. Calhoun's panic at the ostensible power of the Holy Alliance, his interest in the cause of the Greeks, and his inconsistent, emotional statements of the position of the United States are typical of one aspect of public opinion. Adams's nationalism, self-assurance, shrewd judgment, and more harmonious suggestions represent the other phase of the national spirit. Between these two men stood Monroe, exerting a moderating influence on both, reflecting at times the views of each, and ultimately making the decision upon which the policy was to be based. That he chose the more independent, the more nationalistic, and the more fearless course is a tribute both to his own insight and to Adams's arguments. Finally, these cabinet discussions reveal in the clearest way how considerations of American foreign policy at this time revolved around the question of English policy. That she might become involved through fear or self-interest, that her action might injure the United States, and that trouble of any sort between the Old World and the New might result in the complete commercial and political dominance of England, were possibilities which colored all the conversations. . . .

England was the key Power in the formation of American foreign policy. This idea has been traced in some detail, and it should be recalled here that even those who advocated joining her in a declaration of policy did so principally because they sought a means of protecting their country from her hostility. The Holy Alliance was hardly an active menace, and the statements concerning it were motivated more by American nationalism than by fear.

It has been the fashion of late to minimize the importance of the Monroe Doctrine, to rank it as a less brilliant achievement than the Florida treaty of 1819 or the recognition of South America in 1822. Viewed in the light of world politics and the realities of America's position, it appears in a different guise. Regarded for what it really was, it represents the outmaneuvering of a strong Power by a weak one. It made plain to England that war would probably result from further extensions of her political influence in the New World. Either she must fight or renounce the idea of possessing Cuba and establishing new posts in the Oregon country. The Monroe Doctrine was no guaranty of protection to the United States, but it did make the policy of this country clear to all who chose to read. The dangers of foreign connections were avoided, the United States remained free, and England was caught in the mesh of her own tangled policy. The English government was blocked not only by the threat contained in the Monroe Doctrine but also by the fact that the declaration appealed to the widespread sentiments of the masses of the English people. When it is compared with earlier diplomatic successes, the Monroe Doctrine does not suffer. Previously, the United States had been dealing with weak Powers like Spain, or with land Powers like France and Russia. Now, she was primarily concerned with a great sea Power which had no strong motives for placating its weaker rival. The Monroe Doctrine did not produce all the effects which ardent but uncritical writers have claimed for it, but it did accomplish more than recent critics admit. It was no fourth-rate diplomatic move, but a decisive declaration of fundamental policies.

ARTHUR P. WHITAKER (1895–   ) provides an important corrective to Tatum. He agrees that Anglo-American relations had deteriorated by the autumn of 1823 but he cannot accept Tatum's arguments that the Doctrine was for that reason directed against Great Britain. For Whitaker, the bad relations resulted only in the realization by Monroe and his advisers that a joint declaration with Britain was impossible and that Britain was, indeed, a rival in the New World. He sees the Doctrine as directed against France, the only power capable of invading the former Spanish colonies, and he rests his case on Monroe's own statement made in October 1824. Is Monroe's recollection in the fall of 1824 of events of the preceding year an entirely reliable source?*

To Frustrate France's Plans in South America

We have not . . . discussed the important question of the intent of the Doctrine as proclaimed by Monroe—what, precisely, he meant by it. . . . Against which of the European powers was it primarily aimed?

The question, against which power or powers the Monroe Doctrine was principally aimed, brings us to the consideration of another conspicuous effort to correct Perkins's standard account of the subject. In the latter, as in most of the previous accounts, the Doctrine is represented as having been aimed principally against the Holy Alliance, particularly against France and Russia; but in 1935

Mr. E. H. Tatum published a book in which he argued ingeniously and at length that its target was England herself. His argument, based mainly on circumstantial evidence, runs to the effect that the years 1821–1823 were marked by a rising tide of anti-British sentiment in the United States, which was expressed as early as 1821 by Adams's spectacular Independence Day address; that the so-called menace of the Holy Alliance to America in 1823 was a British invention which did not deceive either Monroe or Adams, both of whom were suspicious of England and convinced of her hostility to the United States; that the real threat

* From Arthur P. Whitaker, *The United States and the Independence of Latin America. 1800–1830*, pp. 492–506. Reprinted without footnotes by permission of The Johns Hopkins Press. Copyright 1941 by The Johns Hopkins Press.

to America in 1823 came not from France, either alone or as the agent of the Holy Alliance, but from England; that all the factors which prompted Monroe's decision to proclaim the Doctrine were related to the central idea that England was not sincere in her offer to join the United States in making the declaration proposed by Canning; that Monroe accordingly decided to make an independent declaration; and that this declaration, the Monroe Doctrine, was intended to prevent "any Power whatsoever" from interfering in the Western Hemisphere, but was aimed primarily against England and above all against England's designs on Cuba.

This novel interpretation of the Monroe Doctrine was effectively criticized by Perkins [in his review of Tatum's book in *American Historical Review*, XLII (1936), 156–157], who pointed out among other things how the record of the cabinet discussions of November 1823 and the terms of the Doctrine itself show that it was aimed primarily against the Continental powers. He also pointed out that the warning to Europe, which spread a mantle of protection over the independent states of Spanish America, could not have been aimed at England's designs on Cuba, which was still a colony.

At another point—and it is one of very considerable importance—Perkins's rebuttal was much less effective. He undertook to show that the tide of anti-British feeling in the United States had begun to recede by the early part of 1823 and that, although there was still some remnant of this feeling in administration circles in the latter part of that year, it was not an important factor in the November discussions in which the Doctrine was framed. On this point Tatum seems to be nearer the truth than Perkins, and

the former's position is supported by a piece of evidence the importance of which has not been duly appreciated.

This evidence is furnished by Richard Rush's despatch No. 336 of October 10, 1823,[1] which was received at the State Department on November 16,[2] at the beginning of the momentous series of Cabinet discussions out of which the Monroe Doctrine emerged. . . . This despatch eliminated Canning's proposal for a joint declaration from practical consideration by showing that he was no longer interested in it; but the despatch contained other information of an even more disturbing character. For it not only showed that Canning had abandoned his overtures for cooperation with the United States but also created a strong presumption that he was reverting to the earlier policy of cooperation with the Holy Alliance and to the earlier attitude of indifference if not antagonism towards the United States.

In other words, throughout virtually the whole critical period of the formulation of the Monroe Doctrine the dominant feeling in administrative circles was not one of trust in England based upon Canning's desire for cooperation but of vigorously reawakened suspicion of England based upon Rush's despatch of October 10, 1823. Canning's subsequent course confirmed Rush in his main conclusions. Returning to the United States in 1825 he became a leading member of Adams's Cabinet, as Secretary of the Treasury, and while he held that position

[1] Portions of the despatch are printed in the Tatum selection, pages 30–31, and on pages 36–37 of this selection.—*Ed.*

[2] Tatum (p. 30) states that this despatch was received on November 19. His source is the notation on the first page of the despatch. Whitaker, however, in dating the receipt November 19 used Adams' *Memoirs* (VI, 187), which note the date as the 16th.—*Ed.*

he again asserted the opinion, formed as the result of Canning's tergiversation in the autumn of 1823 and forcefully expressed in his despatch of October 10, 1823, that Canning's policy was essentially antagonistic towards the United States. As this view was one that Adams, the head of the new administration, was predisposed to accept, the effect of the despatch endured long after the end of the crisis to which it related.

The despatch is, therefore, worth quoting at length. It is one of the most important that Rush ever wrote, and obviously more important for the history of the Monroe Doctrine than the earlier despatches in which he reported Canning's desire for cooperation with the United States. It deserves full quotation all the more because it paints Rush's antipathy towards the British government in far livelier colors than those that he used in his memoirs, which were published a score of years later in an effort to improve Anglo-American relations and which appear to have been the main reliance of most historians of this subject. The despatch records the views that Rush held and communicated confidentially to his government in October 1823 and not those that he deemed it fitting to publish under very different circumstances many years later.

Rush began his despatch of October 10 by telling how, although he had seen Canning twice in the past two days, the latter had "said not one single word relative to South America," although the second occasion had been "altogether favorable for resuming the topick." After suggesting that the questions involved in their earlier discussions of August and September might have been essentially changed by the favorable news just received from South America (news of the

surrender of the last Spanish army in Colombia), he continued:

The termination of the discussion between us may be thought somewhat sudden, not to say abrupt, considering how zealously as well as spontaneously it was started on his his [Canning's] side. As I did not commence it, it is not my intention to revive it.

Canning's pointed silence was all the more disturbing because Rush had been expecting him to resume the topic ever since their last discussion of it on September 26. He suspected (as was the case) that it might have been "fresh explanations" with France that had brought Canning to "so full and sudden a pause with me"; and he was certain that nothing had been accomplished by his discussions with the latter.

Canning and I [he wrote] stand as we were before his first advance to me, except for the light our discussions may have shed on the dispositions and policy of England. It appears that having ends of her own in view, she has been anxious to facilitate their accomplishment by invoking my auxiliary offices . . . but as to the independence of the new states of America, for their own benefit, that this seems quite another question in her diplomacy. It is France that must not be aggrandized, not South America that must be made free.

After suggesting that Canning would never renew the discussions unless England needed the aid of the United States for her "schemes of counteraction against France or Russia," he delivered himself of as hot a blast against the British governing class as was ever penned by an American official in that generation.

That the British cabinet, and the governing portion of the British nation, will rejoice at heart in the downfall of the constitutional system in Spain [wrote Rush], I have never had a doubt and have not now, so long as this catastrophe can be kept from crossing the path of British interests and British ambition. This nation, in its collective, corporate, capacity has no more sympathy with popular rights and freedom now, than it had on the plains of Lexington in America; than it showed during the whole progress of the French revolution in Europe, or at the close of its first great act, at Vienna, in 1815; than it exhibited lately at Naples in proclaiming a neutrality in all other events, save that of the safety of the royal family there; or, still more recently, when it stood aloof whilst France and the Holy Alliance avowed their intention of crushing the liberties of unoffending Spain. . . . With a king in the hands of his ministers, with an aristocracy of unbounded opulence and pride, with what is called a house of commons constituted essentially by this aristocracy and always moved by its influence, England can, in reality, never look with complacency upon popular and equal rights, whether abroad or at home. She therefore moves in her natural orbit when she wars, positively or negatively, against them. For their own sakes alone, she will never war in their favor.

Rush concluded his despatch with a disturbing bit of information about British activities in Latin America: the British government was sending consuls to some of the Spanish American countries, but to Mexico it was sending three commissioners, one of whom, according to Canning himself, might remain there as minister. Why, asked Rush, had Britain singled Mexico out for such "provisionary" diplomatic representation? Was it because Mexico had rich mines and a large population, or because of its proximity to the United States?

Bristling with dislike of England's governing class and distrust of her government, Rush's despatch had an effect upon the cabinet discussions of late November which is easier to sense than to measure, but which must have been powerful. At two points its effect is entirely clear and precise. In the first place . . . by showing that Canning had in effect abandoned his proposal of a joint declaration, it left the administration with the alternative of issuing a unilateral declaration or none at all. In the second place, it confirmed Adams in his belief that the British government's alarm over the designs of the Holy Alliance against Spanish America was pretended and that the real purpose of Canning's proposal was to keep the United States from acquiring Cuba.

The most unequivocal evidence of the effect of Rush's despatch on the administration before Monroe's message was communicated to Congress is contained in Adams's reply of November 30. It had been observed, said Adams, that in all his conferences and correspondence with Rush on this subject, Canning

did not disclose the specific information on which he apprehended so immediate an interposition of the European Allies, in the affairs of South America, as would have warranted or required the measure which he proposed to be taken in concert with you, before this Government could be advised of it. *And this remark has drawn the more attention, upon observing the apparent coolness and comparative indifference with which he treated the subject at your last conferences after the peculiar earnestness and solemnity of his first advances.* It would have been more satisfactory here, and would have afforded more distinct light for deliberation, if the confidence in which his proposals originated had at once been entire. This suggestion is now made with a view to the future. . . .[3]

Beyond this we can only say with cer-

---

[3] The italics are inserted by Whitaker.—*Ed.*

tainty that the despatch contained information and advice that pointed towards the decision finally reached by Monroe in consultation with his cabinet. It strengthened the case for a "purely American" policy, for it emphasized the fact that England, the only European power with which the United States might conceivably cooperate, was controlled by a governing class which was scarcely more sympathetic to the political ideals of the United States than were the Holy Allies themselves. It also contained a sharp reminder that in Latin America the chief rival of the United States was not France or any other Continental power, but England. The latter fact also strengthened the case in favor of a strongly worded pronouncement which, even at the risk of war, would maintain the prestige of the United States in the new Spanish American states lest, as Adams said, they should fall so completely under the influence of Britain as to become in effect British colonies.

This is not to say that Monroe was induced, either through Rush's despatch or otherwise, to aim his declaration against Britain, which came within its range only as a part of the European system from which Monroe proclaimed the severance of the American system. What Rush's despatch did was to remind the administration, strongly and at a crucial moment, that Britain was essentially a part of the European system.

Further evidence that the Monroe Doctrine was not directed primarily against British designs on Cuba or on Latin America at large is furnished by Monroe's own statement that it was directed primarily against France. This evidence seems to have escaped the attention of many students of the question;

but that is not surprising, for it is contained in a report by a diplomatic agent of the Buenos Aires government, General Carlos de Alvear, which has not been easily accessible in the northern hemisphere. It was not written by Monroe himself, but it is probably trustworthy since it is based on a long interview that Alvear and his secretary had with Monroe in October 1824, and the conversation was carried on in Spanish (which Monroe had learned in Spain) and was recorded at the time, and, we have no reason to doubt, was reported in good faith and with substantial accuracy. It was held at the instance of Alvear, who wanted to get an authoritative statement of the foreign policy of the United States, and most of the report is devoted to Monroe's remarks on that subject. Its opening sentence bears directly on the question before us:

The President [Monroe] said that fearing that France, after its success in Spain, might undertake an expedition against South America, he made the solemn declaration contained in his annual message of 1823, by which he committed himself in an unequivocal manner to protect the cause of the new states of America in the case referred to in that message; and that he also required the English government to state what course it would follow in case any other nation than Spain should undertake to intervene in the subjugation of the former colonies . . . that the British government replied in a most satisfactory manner through the declaration and speeches of Mr. Canning in Parliament, adopting the principle established by the government of the United States [in Monroe's message] and thereby disconcerting completely the hostile plans of France. . . .

Except that (for easily understandable reasons) Monroe omitted to mention Canning's proposal, its abandonment, and the atmosphere of suspicion of

England in which the Doctrine was formulated, his statement to Alvear is supported by the available evidence. There are two points in it that require special emphasis. In the first place, it states categorically that the warning to Europe was directed at France and was designed to prevent the military intervention of France against the new states of Spanish America. In the second place, it shows Monroe's understanding of the significance of his pronouncement in Anglo-American relations: whereas the acceptance of Canning's proposal would have made the United States the junior partner of Great Britain in Spanish American affairs, Monroe's unilateral declaration and its subsequent support (as Monroe claimed) by Canning reversed the roles and yet (though Monroe did not point this out to Alvear) left the United States with entire freedom of action in regard to both Spanish America and Europe, including England.

Russia, too, played an important role (though one which was subordinate to that of France) in the cabinet discussions of the second part of the Doctrine. It did so mainly because the Russian notes received at Washington in October and November 1823 had made the Tsar seem the ideological champion of the Holy Alliance, although there was also some apprehension that Russia might give military support to French intervention in Spanish America. It was the general sense of the Cabinet that the situation called for a direct reply to the monarchical manifesto from St. Petersburg; but there was considerable difference of opinion as to the tone that should be given to the reply. Adams had an extraordinarily robust faith in the Tsar's essential goodness and liberalism—a faith which perhaps rested on the kindness shown him by the Tsar when he was minister at St. Petersburg and which resisted the efforts of Gallatin (now back from France) to convince him that the Tsar had long since forgotten the liberalism of his salad days.

Adams therefore believed that his great and good friend's present course was the result of a temporary aberration and that a verbal chastisement might be enough to bring him back into the path of rectitude. The note that he drafted for this purpose was not a little remarkable, for its language was so provocative that it startled even those members of the Cabinet who were much less well disposed towards the Tsar than Adams. Wirt called one passage in it a "hornet of a paragraph." Monroe himself counselled moderation, and in the end Adams again yielded to his chief, though most reluctantly. The upshot of all these discussions was a much milder reply to Russia than the one Adams had proposed to make.

WORTHINGTON C. FORD (1858–1941), distinguished historian, archivist, and editor of the writings of John Quincy Adams, gives Adams all the credit for the Monroe Doctrine. He was the first person to stress Adams' role in the formulation of the Doctrine. He bases his view on an examination of Adams' drafts, as revealed in Adams' *Memoirs*, of two of the most important documents relating to the Monroe message, the instructions to Rush and the reply to Tuyll, and Monroe's amendments and changes. In Adams' draft, he claims, may be seen all the ideas that came to be the Monroe Doctrine. How does this view fit in with MacCorkle's argument that the essential ideas were expressed earlier by Monroe in his letters to Jefferson and Madison?*

The Work of John Quincy Adams

On November 13 Adams prepared the usual memorandum of suggestions for the President's annual message at the opening of the session of Congress.[1] He took it to the Executive Mansion and found Monroe "still altogether unsettled in his own mind" on the answer to be given to Canning's proposals, and "alarmed, far beyond anything that I could have conceived possible, with the fear that the Holy Alliance are about to restore immediately all South America to Spain." In this view he was supported by Calhoun, a man who certainly did not err on the side of a cheerful optimism, and the surrender of Cadiz to the French was the immediate cause of this despair. Adams pressed for a decision, either to accept or to decline Canning's advances, and a despatch could then be prepared conformable to either decision.[2] Monroe's vacillation was all the more notable as he had received the counsels of

[1] This memorandum is among the Monroe MSS. in the New York Public Library. It consists of four pages of manuscript, and contains nothing on Canning's proposition. I was in the belief that it was an incomplete paper until I found in the Ford collection, in the same library, a rough note in Monroe's writings of "Adams's Sketch," closely following the heads of the Adams manuscript and leaving no doubt of its covering all the points of that paper.

[2] *Memoirs of John Quincy Adams,* VI. 185.

* From Worthington C. Ford, "John Quincy Adams and the Monroe Doctrine," *American Historical Review,* VIII (1902), 28-52. Reprinted by permission of the American Historical Association.

Jefferson and Madison, an episode of which Adams was still in ignorance, for he was not shown the letters until the fifteenth.

If Calhoun was the alarmist member of the Cabinet, Adams was at the other extreme. As well expect Chimborazo to sink beneath the ocean, he believed, as to look to the Holy Alliance to restore the Spanish dominion upon the American continent. If the South Americans really had so fragile governments as Calhoun represented them to be, there was every reason not to involve the United States in their fate. With indecision in the President and dark apprehension in Calhoun, Adams alone held a definite opinion, and in clear phrase he expressed it in summation of the Cabinet discussion:

I thought we should bring the whole answer to Mr. Canning's proposals to a test of right and wrong. Considering the South Americans as independent nations, they themselves, and no other nation, had the *right* to dispose of their condition. *We* have no right to dispose of them, either alone or in conjunction with other nations. Neither have any other nations the right of disposing of them without their consent. This principle will give us a clue to answer all Mr. Canning's questions with candor and confidence, and I am to draft a dispatch accordingly."[3]

At this juncture Russia again intervened. On November 15, Baron de Tuyll communicated to Adams extracts from a despatch received from his court, dated August 30, N. S., containing an exposition of the views of the Emperor Alexander and his allies on the affairs of Spain and Portugal.[4] . . .

This remarkable manifesto,[5] most appropriate for an autocrat in speaking to other autocrats, but entirely unsuited

for gaining the confidence of the "one example of a successful democratic rebellion," naturally influenced Adams in preparing his reply to Canning. The draft of a despatch on all the communications from Rush bearing upon the proposed concert was prepared on November 17, and given to the President on the same day. Whatever may have been the general intention of Adams in preparing this draft, the scope of his policy was greatly enlarged by the communications made by the Russian minister. It was sufficiently aggravating to have been lectured on political principles in the note instructing the minister to make it known that the Emperor would receive no representatives from the late Spanish colonies.[6] . . . But now another Russian manifesto had been communicated, explaining more fully, and, it may be added, more offensively, the views and intentions of the Holy Alliance, couched in language which only an autocrat could employ. It was the Holy Alliance proclaiming the virtues and glories of despotism. This gave Adams his opening. If the Emperor set up to be the mouthpiece of Divine Providence, it would be well to intimate that this country did not recognize the language spoken, and had a destiny of its own, also under the guidance of Divine Providence. If Alexander could exploit his political principles, those of a brutal repressive policy, the United States could show

[3] *Memoirs of John Quincy Adams,* VI. 186.

[4] The despatch, which Ford prints in the original French, describes the victories of the allies in Spain in putting down the revolution there. Adams called it "an *Io Triumphe* over the fallen cause of revolution" and Ford later (p. 44) called it a "paean on despotism."—*Ed.*

[5] Ford calls the despatch a manifesto because it also proclaimed the intention of the Continental allies to suppress all future revolutions.—*Ed.*

[6] This note was dated October 16, 1823.—*Ed.*

that another system of government, remote and separate from European traditions and administration, could give rise to a new and more active political principle—the consent of the governed, between which and the Emperor there could not exist even a sentimental sympathy. If the Holy Alliance could boast of its strength and agreement when engaged in stamping out all opposition to legitimacy, the United States, hearing the whisperings of a projected American union, with itself at the head, an Alliance that did not arrogate to itself the epithet of Holy, could demand that the European concert justify its existence, its actions and its motives by records other than the bloody scenes at Naples, in France, and in Spain. Here was Adams's opportunity. It was no longer Canning who was to be answered; it was Europe—and he seized it as only a masterful man, certain of his ground, can find in the very reasons of his opponent the best of support for his own position.

In the following parallel are given Adams's first draft of the answer to Canning, prepared November 17, and the amendments made by Monroe, November 20.

Adams's Draft[7]

N. 76 Richard Rush, Envoy Extraordinary and Minister Plenipotentiary, U. S., London.

Department of State Washington,
29 November, 1823

. . . That we could not see with indifference any attempt [by one or more powers of Europe to dispose of the Freedom or Independence of those States, without their consent, or against their will.]

[To this principle, in our view of this subject all the rest are subordinate. Without this, our concurrence with Great-Britain upon all the rest would be useless.] It is upon this ground alone as we conceive that a firm and determined stand could now be jointly taken by Great Britain and the United States in behalf of the *Independence of Nations,* and never in the History of Mankind was there a period when a stand

[*Monroe's Amendments*]

substitute the following after attempt. . . .

"any attempt by one or more powers of Europe, to restore those new States, to the crown of Spain, or to deprive them, in any manner whatever, of the freedom and independence which they have acquired, [*Much less could we behold with indifference the transfer of those new gov^{ts}., or of any portion of the spanish possessions, to other powers, especially of the territories, bordering on, or nearest to the UStates.*"]

omit in next parg^h. the passage marked and substitute the following—

"with a view to this object, it is indispensable that the British gov^t. take like ground, with that which is now held by the UStates,—that it recognize the independence of the new gov^{ts}.—That measure being taken, we may then harmonize, in all the [*necessary*] arrangements and acts, which may be necessary for its accomplishment." [*the object.*] It is upon this ground alone, etc. [*to the end of the parag^h.*]

[7] What is inclosed in brackets of both Adams's and Monroe's papers was omitted in the final form of this despatch.

so taken and maintained, would exhibit to present and future ages a more glorious example of Power, animated by Justice and devoted to the ends of beneficence.

[With the addition of this principle, if assented to by the British Government, you are authorised to join in any act formal or informal, which shall manifest the concurrence of the two Governments on this momentous occasion. But you will explicitly state that without this basis of Right and moral obligation, we can see no foundation upon which the concurrent action of the two Governments can be harmonized.

If the destinies of South America, are to be trucked and bartered between Spain and her European Allies, by amicable negotiation, or otherwise, without consulting the feelings or the rights of the People who inhabit that portion of our Hemisphere.]

[The ground of Resistance which we would oppose to any *interference* of the European Allies, between Spain and South America, is not founded on any partial interest of our own or of others. If the Colonies belonged to Spain we should object to any transfer of them to other Nations, which would materially affect our interests or rights, but with that exception we should consider Spain as possessing the common Power of disposing of her own Territories. Our present opposition to the disposal of any part of the American Continents by Spain, with her European allies is that they do not belong to Spain, and can no more be disposed of by her, than by the United States.

With regard to the Islands of Cuba and Porto-Rico, to the Inhabitants of which the free Constitution of Spain, as accepted and sworn to by the King has been extended, we consider them as possessing the right of determining for themselves their course of conduct, under the subversion of that constitution, by foreign Military power. Our own interest and wish would be that they should continue in their political connection with Spain under the administration of a free

omit the residue and substitute something like the following—

["We have no intention of acquiring any portion of the spanish possessions for ourselves, nor shall we ever do it by force. Cuba is that portion, the admission of which into our union, would be the most eligible, but it is the wish of this gov^t., that it remain, at least for the present, attached to Spain. We have declared this sentiment publickly. and shall continue to act on it. It could not be admitted into our union, unless it should first declare its independence, and that independence should be acknowledged by Spain, events which may not occur for a great length of time, and which the UStates will rather discourage than promote.]

On this basis, this gov^t. is willing to move in concert with G. Britain, for the purposes specified.

[with a view however to that object, it [*is submitted*] merits consideration, whether it will not [*be most advantageous to*] contribute most effectually, to its accomplishment, a perfect understanding being established between the two gov^{ts}., that they act for the present, & until some eminent danger should occur, separately, each making such representation to the allied powers, or to either of them as shall be deemd most advisable. Since the receipt of your letters, a communication has been made by Baron T. the Russian minister here, to the following effect. [then state his letter respecting minister etc., and also the informal communication. State also the instructions given to M^r. Middleton, and *those* the purport of those, which will be given to the minister at Paris.] On this subject, it will be proper for you to communicate freely with Mr. Canning, as to ascertain fully the sentiments of his gov^t. He will doubtless be explicit, as to the danger of any movement of the allied powers, or of any,

Constitution, and in the enjoyment of their Liberties as now possessed; we could not see them transferred to any other Power, or subjected to the antient and exploded dominion of Spain, with indifference. We aim not at the possession of them ourselves.]

I am with great Respect, Sir, your very humble and obed' Serv'. . . .

or either of them, for the subjugation, or transfer of any portion of the territory in question, from Spain, to any other power. If there be no such danger, there will be no motive for such concert, and it is only on satisfactory proof of that danger, that you are authorized to provide for it.]

On November 21st these papers were examined in Cabinet meeting. Canning had said that Great Britain would not throw any impediment in the way of an arrangement between the colonies and mother country, by amicable negotiation. He would not object to the colonies, under that method, granting to Spain commercial privileges greater than those given to other nations. This did not meet the wishes of Adams, who desired for the United States the footing of the most favored nation. The President did not understand the full meaning of this wish, and proposed a modifying amendment, "which seemed to admit that we should not object to an arrangement by which special favors, or even a restoration of authority, might be conceded to Spain." This was to accept Canning's position to the full, and perhaps even went further, for the restoration of Spanish authority could hardly have occurred to a man who started from the belief that the recovery of the colonies by Spain was hopeless. Both Calhoun and Adams strenuously objected. "The President ultimately acceded to the substance of the phrase as I had in the first instance made the draft; but finally required that the phraseology of it should be varied. Almost all the other amendments proposed by the President were opposed principally by Mr. Calhoun, who most explicitly preferred my last substituted

paragraph to the President's projected amendment. The President did not insist upon any of his amendments which were not admitted by general consent, and the final paper, though considerably varied from my original draft, will be conformable to my own views."[8]

One paper still remained to be answered, and it was really the most important of all—the Emperor's paean on despotism. Not only was it important as an expression of opinions and policy abhorrent to the American system of government, but it gave Adams the opportunity of making a reply to Europe. Canning's offer of a joint responsibility, limited it must be added to furthering the ends of Great Britain, was no longer to be considered. As an ally of Great Britain the United States would play a very secondary part. Alone, even against united Europe, America could gain the same result and without departing from a policy of avoiding entangling political alliances with any European power. Monroe was willing to raise a European question by aiding Spain and Greece. Adams avoided such a step and changed the issue into an American question, to be determined by America without the interference of any European government, whether English or continental. In this lies the great merit and strength of Adams's position. He lifted the ques-

[8] *Memoirs of John Quincy Adams*, VI. 193.

tion from one of joint action with England to one of individual action of the United States.

At the Cabinet meeting of November 21, Adams outlined his intended reply to the later communications received from Baron Tuyll, a paper to be first communicated verbally and afterwards delivered to him confidentially. "My purpose would be in a moderate and conciliatory manner, but with a firm and determined spirit, to declare our dissent from the principles avowed in those communications; to assert those upon which our own Government is founded, and, while disclaiming all intention of attempting to propagate them by force, and all interference with the political affairs of Europe, to declare our expectation and hope that the European powers will equally abstain from the attempt to spread their principles in the American hemisphere, or to subjugate by force any part of these continents to their will."[9]

While the President approved this idea, his first draft of his message to Congress showed that he had not comprehended the general drift of the Secretary's intentions in the conduct of the foreign relations of the United States. In [his letter of the same day] calling the Cabinet meeting for the 21st he had included among the questions to be considered "whether any, and if any, what notice, shall be taken of Greece, and also of the invasion of Spain by France."[10] Accordingly his draft alluded to recent events in Spain and Portugal, "speaking in terms of the most pointed reprobation of the late invasion of Spain by France, and of the principles upon which it was undertaken by the open avowal of the King of France. It also contained a broad acknowledgment of the Greeks as an independent nation."[11] Where was the

future Monroe doctrine in all this? It was, as Adams said, a call to arms against all Europe, and for objects of policy exclusively European—Greece and Spain. Protest only led the President to promise to draw up two sketches for consideration, conformable to the two different aspects of the subject. He was ready to adopt either, as his Cabinet might advise. Nothing could better prove how the essential part of Adams's views had escaped Monroe's attention. On the next day the Secretary again urged Monroe to abstain from everything in his message which the Holy Alliance could make a pretext for construing into aggression upon them. He should end his administration—"hereafter to be looked back to as the golden age of this republic"—in peace. If the Holy Alliance were determined to make up an issue with the United States, "it was our policy to meet it, and not to make it. . . . If they intend now to interpose by force, we shall have as much as we can do to prevent them, without going to bid them defiance in the heart of Europe."[12] And Adams again stated the heart of his desired policy in unmistakable words: "The ground that I wish to take is that of earnest remonstrance against the interference of

9 *Memoirs of John Quincy Adams*, VI. 194.

10 James Monroe to John Quincy Adams.

Dear Sir,—I have given notice to the other members of the admⁿ., who are present, to meet here at one o clock, at which time you will bring over the draught of the instruction to Mr. Rush for consideration. I mean to bring under consideration, at the same time, the important question, whether any, and if any, what notice, shall be taken of Greece, and also of the invasion of Spain by France. With a view to the latter object, be so good as to bring over with you, a copy of the King's Speech, to the legislative corps, announcing the intended invasion.

Novʳ 21. 1823.   J. M.

11 *Memoirs of John Quincy Adams*, VI. 194.

12 *Memoirs of John Quincy Adams*, VI. 197.

the European powers by force with South America, but to disclaim all interference on our part with Europe; to make an American cause and adhere inflexibly to that." . . . The President modified his paragraphs on foreign affairs, and made them conformable to the spirit of Adams's position. The result is to be seen in the Presidential message of December 2, 1823, enunciating the doctrine that has since gone under the name of Monroe.

Adams had prepared the draft of his reply to the Russian communication, as he thought, in such a manner as to "correspond exactly with a paragraph of the President's message which he had read to me yesterday, and which was entirely conformable to the system of policy which I have earnestly recommended for this emergency." It was intended to be a firm, spirited, and yet conciliatory answer to all the communications lately received from the Russian government, and at the same time an unequivocal answer to the proposals made by Canning to Rush. . . .

How far these intentions were fulfilled a careful study of the paper itself will show. Like all of Adams's papers it is clearly expressed and most direct to the point.

Observations on the Communications recently received from the Minister of Russia.[13]

The Government of the United States of America is *Republican*. By their Constitution it is provided that "The United States shall guaranty to every State in this Union, a *Republican* form of Government, and shall protect each of them from invasion. . . .

[The principles of this form of Polity are; 1 that the Institution of Government, to be lawful, must be pacific, that is founded upon the consent, and by the agreement of those who are governed; and 2 that each Nation

---

[13] What is enclosed between brackets was struck out of the paper.

is exclusively the judge of the Government best suited to itself, and that no other Nation, can justly interfere by force to impose a different Government upon it. The first of these principles may be designated, as the principle of *Liberty*—the second as the principle of National *Independence*—They are both Principles of *Peace* and of Good Will to Men.] . . .

Among the Powers of Europe, Russia is one with whom the United States have entertained the most friendly and mutually beneficial intercourse. Through all the vicissitudes of War and Revolution, of which the world for the last thirty years has been the theatre, the good understanding between the two Governments has been uninterrupted. The Emperor Alexander in particular has not ceased to manifest sentiments of Friendship and good-will to the United States from the period of his accession to the throne, to this moment, and the United States on their part, have as invariably shown the interest which they take in his Friendship and the solicitude with which they wish to retain it.

In the communications recently received from the Baron de Tuyll, so far as they relate to the immediate objects of intercourse between the two Governments, the President sees with high satisfaction, the avowal of unabated cordiality and kindness towards the United States on the part of the Emperor.

With regard to the communications which relate to the Affairs of Spain and Portugal, and to those of South America, while sensible of the candour and frankness with which they are made, the President indulges the hope, that they are not intended *either* to mark an Æra either of change, in the friendly dispositions of the Emperor towards the United States or of hostility to the principles upon which their Governments are founded; or of deviation from the system of neutrality hitherto observed by him and his allies, in the contest between Spain and America.

To the Notification that the Emperor, in conformity with the *political principles* maintained by himself and his Allies, has determined to receive no Agent from any of the Governments *de facto,* which have been recently formed in the new World it has been thought sufficient to answer that the United States, faithful to *their* political principles, have recognised and now consider them as the Governments of Independent Nations.

To the signification of the Emperor's hope and desire that the United States should continue to observe the neutrality which they have proclaimed between Spain and South-America, the answer has been that the Neutrality of the United States will be maintained, as long as that of Europe, apart from Spain, shall continue and that they hope that of the Imperial Government of Russia will be continued.

[To the confidential communication from the Baron de Tuyll, of the Extract, dated Sᵗ. Petersburg 30 August 1823. So far as it relates to the affairs of Spain and Portugal, the only remark which it is thought necessary to make, is of the great satisfaction with which the President has noticed *that* paragraph, which contains the frank and solemn admissions that *"the undertaking of the Allies, yet demands a last Apology to the eyes of Europe."*]

In the general declarations that the allied Monarchs will never compound, and never will even treat with the *Revolution* and that their policy has only for its object by *forcible* interposition to guaranty the tranquility of *all the States of which the civilised world is composed,* the President wishes to perceive sentiments, the application of which is limited, and intended in their results to be limited to the Affairs of Europe.

That the sphere of their operations was not intended to embrace the United States of America, nor any portion of the American Hemisphere.

And finally deeply desirous as the United States are of preserving the general peace of the world, their friendly intercourse with all the European Nations, and especially the most cordial harmony and good-will with the Imperial Government of Russia, it is due as well to their own unalterable Sentiments, as to the explicit avowal of them, called for

by the communications received from the Baron de Tuyll, to declare

That the United States of America, and their Government, could not see with indifference, the forcible interposition of any European Power, other than Spain, either to restore the dominion of Spain over her emancipated Colonies in America, or to establish Monarchical Governments in those Countries or to transfer any of the possessions heretofore or yet subject to Spain in the American Hemisphere, to any other European Power.

> Department of State Washington,
> 27 November, 1823

When Adams laid before the Cabinet on the twenty-fifth this draft of his paper, much discussion and opposition were developed. The timidity of Monroe was aroused, and the other members of the Cabinet hesitated. Calhoun questioned whether it would be proper to deliver any such paper to the Russian minister; it contained an ostentatious display of republican principles, might be offensive to the Russian government, and even to that of Great Britain, which would by no means relish so much republicanism. The President's message would be sufficient. "It was a mere communication to our own people. Foreign powers might not feel themselves bound to notice what was said in that. It was like a family talking over subjects interesting to them by the fireside among themselves. Many things might be said there without offense, even if a stranger should come among them and overhear the conversation, which would be offensive if they went to his house to say them."[14]

Wirt, the Attorney-General, raised the point whether the United States would be justified in taking so broadly the ground of resistance to the interposition

[14] *Memoirs of John Quincy Adams,* **VI.** 200.

of the Holy Alliance by force to restore the Spanish dominion in South America. If the Holy Alliance should act in direct hostility against South America, would this country oppose them by war? There was danger in assuming the attitude of menace without meaning to strike. But Adams, while admitting the remote possibility of war, saw no immediate prospect of that event: "The interest of no one of the allied powers would be promoted by the restoration of South America to Spain; that the interest of each one of them was against it, and that if they could possibly agree among themselves upon a partition principle, the only possible bait they could offer to Great Britain for acceding to it was Cuba, which neither they nor Spain would consent to give her; that my reliance upon the co-operation of Great Britain rested not upon her principles, but her interest."[15]

Calhoun was filled with gloomy apprehensions. Having subdued South America, the Allies would turn their attention to the United States, "to put down what had been called the first example of successful democratic rebellion." By taking a firm stand now these intentions might be frustrated, even at the expense of war. And he repeated his suggestion of answering the Russian communications by the paragraph in the Presidential message. To this Adams gave a conclusive reply.

The communications from the Russian Minister required a direct and explicit answer. A communication of the paragraph in the President's message would be no answer, and if given as an answer would certainly be very inconsistent with the position that foreigners have no right to notice it, because it was all said among ourselves.[16] . . .

For three days the discussion was continued, and resulted finally in a victory for Adams, but at the expense of two paragraphs of his draft—those indicated by the brackets. The Secretary fought well to have them retained, and thought the first of them to be the "heart of his paper." From the principles there given "all the remainder of the paper was drawn. Without them, the rest was a fabric without a foundation." The President[17] was fearful, and Wirt described the paragraph as a "hornet of a paragraph, and, he thought, would be exceedingly offensive." Adams in reply could only say that it was the "cream of my paper," but he felt that the President would not let it pass. Monroe, after forty-eight hours of consideration, gave an opinion:

Nov[r] 27 [1823.]

The direct attack which the parag[h]. makes on the recent movements, of the Emperor, and of course, censure, on him, and its tendency to irritate, suggest the apprehension that it may produce an unfavorable effect. The illustration of our principles, is one thing; the doing it, in such a form, bearing directly, on what has passed, and which is avoided in the message, is another. Nevertheless, as you attach much interest to this passage, I am willing that you insert it, being very averse to your omitting anything w[ch] you deem so material.   J. M.[18]

[16] *Memoirs of John Quincy Adams*, VI. 208.
[17] James Monroe to John Quincy Adams.
Dear Sir,—I am inclined to think that the second parag[h]. had better be omitted, and that such part of the 3[d]. be also omitted, as will make that parag[h]., stand, as the second distinct proposition, in our system. The principle of the paper, will not be affected by this modification, and it will be less likely to produce excitement anywhere.
Two other passages, the first in the first page, and the second, in the 3[d]. are also marked for omission.   J. M.
You had better see the Baron immediately.
Nov[r]. 27, 1823.
[18] From the Adams MSS.

[15] *Memoirs of John Quincy Adams*, VI. 203.

T. R. SCHELLENBERG (1903–   ), for many years assistant archivist of the United States, takes issue with Ford on two counts: the relative importance of the long-range ideas in the Doctrine and authorship. He considers the most significant part of the Doctrine to be the idea of separation from Europe, an idea that he attributes to Thomas Jefferson. Hence, Jefferson is given the greatest credit as originator. For Schellenberg, the ideological antecedents of the Doctrine are more important than the "circumstances which led to its promulgation." He traces the concept of separation, the doctrine's most lasting element, in Jefferson's thought.*

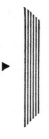

▶

Jefferson Responsible for Basic Doctrine

In considering the immediate origins of the doctrine . . . there has been a tendency to emphasize the circumstances which led to its promulgation to the neglect of the intellectual processes by which the doctrine came to take the exact form that it did and particularly to the neglect of the contributions made by the several statesmen involved to the sense of the final form. From this angle, further light can still be shed on the origins of the Monroe Doctrine.

In evaluating the relative parts played, in the formulation of the Monroe Doctrine, by John Quincy Adams, the staunch New Englander in the depart-

ment of state, and by the three Virginians, Monroe, Jefferson, and Madison, each on his own hill-top pondering the momentous question presented by the overtures of the British foreign secretary, the former has been given chief credit. Adams has had able champions, though none more able than himself. The influence of Jefferson, on the other hand, has not been sufficiently appreciated.

The essential principles of the Monroe Doctrine are found, as is well known, in two different parts of the presidential message of December 2, 1823. In the first part of the message is found the principle

* From T. R. Schellenberg, "Jeffersonian Origins of the Monroe Doctrine," *Hispanic American Historical Review*, XIV (1934), 1-32. Reprinted without footnotes by permission of the author and Duke University Press.

that colonization in America must cease. For this principle Adams is unquestionably responsible. The more general principles, embodying the doctrine of two spheres of political action, one exclusively European and the other exclusively American, occur in the latter part of the message, and there is reason to think that these are derived from the thought of Thomas Jefferson more than from any other source.

Non-intervention by the United States in European affairs had been a cardinal principle of American foreign policy from the first, and Jefferson had always drawn a line of distinction between the political interests of Europe and those of America. Thomas Paine, in his *Common Sense,* was probably the first to state the principle explicitly when he said: "It is to the true interests of America to steer clear of European contentions." This principle was immediately adopted as a political maxim of which Jefferson became a principal exponent. It formed the first tenet in his American system of policy, to which he gradually added the supplementary principle that Europe must keep out of America. In various of his letters one finds in embryo the doctrine of two spheres. Jefferson's ideas, so long in germinating, did not fully emerge, however, until his final retirement to Monticello. Coming to his Virginia estate in the spring of 1809, a white-haired man of sixty-three years, to escape the turmoil of political life, Jefferson became more concerned with broad outlines of American policy than with its intricate details. Having no longer an active share in the direction of foreign relations, his knowledge of them was gleaned from the *Richmond Enquirer,* which was the only newspaper that he took, from such books on the foreign situation as came to his hands, and from

such contacts as he had with men of affairs through their letters to him and through their occasional visits to Monticello.

Among the intellectual influences which served to crystallize Jefferson's ideas on a peculiar American policy into the doctrine of two spheres, the writings of a second-rate French publicist, upon whom Jefferson lavished some of his inexhaustible interest, must hold first place.

Early in 1819, almost five years before the pronouncement of the Monroe Doctrine, a Frenchman formulated, in words as clear and definite as those of the document itself, its two fundamental principles, predicting that they would form the basis of an American system of policy, clearly distinct from that of the old world. The Abbé Dominique-Georges-Frédéric de Riom de Prolhiac de Fourt de Pradt, as prolific in writings as he is well-supplied with names, developed his ideas of American policy in a series of some fourteen books on American affairs published from 1817 to 1828. A number of these are known to have engaged the attention of Thomas Jefferson. The first, entitled *Des Colonies et de la Révolution actuelle de l'Amérique,* Jefferson found both "eloquent" and "ingenious." The most significant, however, from the standpoint of its influence upon Jefferson, was his *L'Europe après le Congrès d'Aix-la-Chapelle, faisant suite au Congrès de Vienne,* which appeared in 1819. Another of his books, *L'Europe et l'Amérique en 1821,* published in 1822, was also in the possession of Jefferson.

In all these books, Pradt emphasized the importance of new world movements, the clear line of cleavage between the new world and the old, and the opposing political systems of the two. In his *L'Europe et l'Amérique en 1821,* in which he devoted a whole section to a discussion of purely American affairs, he wrote:

I have for a long time, drawn the attention to, and shewn the world on the other side of the Atlantic in opposition to Europe, and forming to itself a system, from which a contrast to the institutions, by which Europe is governed, will result, which must attract the observation of every one.

Jefferson, ever sympathetic toward French political thought, was made acquainted with Pradt's *L'Europe après le Congrès d'Aix-la-Chapelle* by its translator. In 1820, the year after the appearance of the French edition, an English translation by George Alexander Otis was published at Philadelphia. The book, through its discussion of the European congress that coincidentally defined the principles of the concert of powers and illustrated its attitude toward American affairs, seems to have profoundly influenced Jefferson's conception of the political system of the old world. Its ideas as to American policy seem also to have made a definite impression. In it, Pradt wrote:

There arises beyond the sea, as did Carthage opposite to Rome, a power which tends to form *an American system;* exclusive of all European influence. This system is evidently that of the *United States.* It cannot fail to become that also of all the states, which strive to form themselves throughout the extent of this country. This plan leads America to two things. 1. To abstain from all participation in the affairs of Europe. 2. To prohibit Europe all participation in the affairs of America. This is a primary, elementary datum, destined to form the basis of American policy, and to keep it separate from that of Europe. It consists in reciprocity of independence; and merely signifies the intention to abstain, that others may abstain; to respect, in order to be respected in turn. . . . It is evident that this

aversion from all participation with European policy is an axiom for the United States, and is destined to become that of all America.[1]

It is, of course, impossible to establish with certainty the extent and manner of Pradt's influence upon Jefferson, and yet this influence is as probable as it has been unsuspected. Jefferson's interest in Pradt's books, and his tendency, quite natural in itself, to attach importance to those writings that confirmed his views, make Pradt's penetrating delineation of an American system an influence that must be taken into account.

Jefferson, as already noted, had long recognized the first of the principles stated by Pradt that America should abstain from all participation in the affairs of Europe. Various causes made it natural and inevitable that the converse of this policy—of European nonintervention in Aemrica—should develop. It was necessary, however, to formulate and state this supplementary principle, the principle that it was the natural province of the United States, as the leading American power, to keep Europe from interfering in the affairs of America. Pradt was probably the first to do this. His penetrating assertion that the two principles were the "primary, elementary datum, destined to form the basis of American policy" could not have failed to influence Jefferson. Though Pradt may not have originally implanted the ideas of an American system in Jefferson's mind, it is almost certain that he served to crystallize Jefferson's views in regard to it. The influence of Pradt is reflected in various ways.

Two letters by Jefferson, both indicating that his views in regard to American policy may have been affected, contain

[1] Italics supplied by translator of de Pradt. —*Ed.*

direct references to the book on the Congress of Aix-la-Chapelle. Shortly after receiving the book, on July 8, 1820, Jefferson wrote to Otis, the translator:

I thank you for De Pradt's book on the Congress of Aix-la-Chapelle—it is a work I had never seen, and had much wished to see. Altho [sic] his style has too much of amphibology to be suited to the sober precision of Politics, yet we gather from him great outlines, and profound views of the new constitution of Europe and of its probable consequences. Those are things we should understand to know how to keep clear of them.

Almost two years later, Jefferson, still impressed by the clairvoyant character of Pradt's book, revealed its effect upon himself. On March 2, 1822, in a letter to Edward Everett, in thanking him for a copy of a book written by Everett's brother, Jefferson observed:

Tossed at random on an ocean of uncertainties and falsehoods, it is joyful at times to catch the glimmering of a beacon which shows us truly where we are. De Pradt's Europe had some effect in this way; but the less as the author was the less known in character.

Indirectly also Jefferson revealed the probable influence of Pradt's *L'Europe après le Congrès d'Aix-la-Chapelle.* Shortly after receiving the book, Jefferson made a proposal of an American system to the Abbé José-Francisco Corréa da Serra, a Portuguese naturalist to whom he was warmly attached, and who was appointed minister plenipotentiary of Portugal, and also to President Monroe. As Portuguese minister, Corréa was chiefly concerned with the suppression of piracies committed on Portuguese vessels under commissions and letters of marque issued by José Artigas, the military leader of Banda Oriental, which had broken away from Brazil. Corréa claimed indemnity from the United States government because some of the privateers, he alleged, were fitted out in American ports and manned in part by American citizens. This question troubled Corréa for over five years, and Jefferson, as his friend, shared his vexation. As a solution of the problem, Jefferson suggested in 1820 the adoption of an American system, by which the United States and Portugal, which was an American power because its sovereign was still resident in Brazil, should reach an agreement with the European powers, whereby the former should suppress the piracies of the western hemisphere, while the latter should clear the seas of the eastern hemisphere of the Barbary pirates.

The significance of this proposal by Jefferson has been lost completely, for neither the importance he attached to it nor the solicitations he made in its behalf to the Portuguese minister, Corréa, and to President Monroe have been known. In a letter to his friend William Short, often quoted because it expressed both Jefferson's views on religion and on foreign policy, is found the first statement of the proposed American system. Referring to Corréa's recent visit to Monticello, Jefferson described his system on August 4, 1820, in a style so grandiloquent that whatever practical import it may have had has been obscured. He wrote:

From many conversations with him, I hope he sees, and will promote in his new situation the advantages of a cordial fraternization among all the American nations, and the importance of their coalescing in an American system of policy, totally independent of and unconnected with that of Europe. The day is not distant, when we may formally require a meridian of partition through the ocean which separates the two hemispheres, on the hither side of which no European gun shall ever be heard, nor an American on the other; and when, during the rage of eternal wars of Europe, the lion and the lamb, within our regions, shall lie down together in peace. The excess of population in Europe, and want of room, render war, in their opinion, necessary to keep down that excess of numbers. Here room is abundant, population scanty, and peace the necessary means of life and happiness. The principles of society there and here, then, are radically different, and I hope no American patriot will ever lose sight of the essential policy of interdicting in the seas and territories of both Americas, the ferocious and sanguinary contests of Europe. I wish to see this coalition begun. I am earnest for an agreement with the maritime powers of Europe, assigning them the task of keeping down the piracies of their seas and the cannibalisms of the African coasts, and to us, the suppression of the same enormities within our seas; and for this purpose, I should rejoice to see the fleets of Brazil and the United States riding together as brethren of the same family, and pursuing the same object. And indeed it would be of happy augury to begin at once this concert of action here, on the invitation of either to the other government, while the way might be preparing for withdrawing our cruisers from Europe, and preventing naval collisions there which daily endanger our peace.

The actual attempts Jefferson made to introduce his American system have been overlooked also. The same day this letter was sent to Short, an extract from it was made by Jefferson's ingenious polygraph and was sent to an unknown person, who must be identified as President Monroe, as is obvious from the content of the latter's letter of August 23, 1820, to Jefferson. In later conversations with Monroe and Corréa on the subject, Jefferson urged the necessity of the adoption of his American system. Under the influence of Jefferson, Corréa addressed to the department of state the proposal that Portugal unite with the United States in the formulation of an "American system of politics, in contra-distinction to an European."

The reaction of Adams and Monroe to this proposal is interesting in the light of subsequent events. Adams, the secretary of state, contemptuously recorded in his *Memoirs,* after conversing with Corréa: "As to an American system, we have it; we constitute the whole of it; there is no community of interests or of principles between North and South America." Monroe, however, evidently took into serious consideration Corréa's proposal, which he knew came indirectly from Jefferson. The idea, he wrote to his secretary of state, "has something imposing in it." To Jefferson he wrote, on returning the extract from the letter to William Short:

I return you the extract which you were so kind as to give me the perusal of. . . . The sentiments expressed in favor of an American interest and policy, extended in the first instance to the preservation of order, along our coast, & in our Seas, are sound, and will in all probability ripen into a system, at no distant period.

. . . The intimate relation existing between Jefferson and Monroe is well known. Monroe, when president, leaned heavily for advice in foreign affairs on both the two former presidents, Jefferson and Madison, who were passing their declining years on their Virginia estates of Monticello and Montpelier. Before Monroe became president, his home at Oakwood, a few miles from Monticello, was often the termination of Jefferson's daily rides. When Monroe went to Washington later Jefferson wrote wistfully:

To have terminated it [the daily ride] sometimes at Oakwood with a half-hour's conversation with those whose minds, familiarised with the same scenes would range with sympathy over the same topics would have chequered the monotony of a country life disengaged from country occupation.

Later, while Monroe was president, it was Jefferson's habit to meet him as often as possible to discuss the situation of affairs. "In these short interviews with you," wrote Jefferson retrospectively in June, 1823, "I generally get my political compass rectified, learn from you whereabouts we are, and correct my course again. In exchange for this I can give you but newspaper ideas. . . .", and one may suppose, ideas in regard to the broad outlines of policy which were evolving in his mind.

Monroe's dependence upon Jefferson is apparent in the letter of June, 1823, when the president, failing to meet Jefferson as he had planned, wrote him that he regretted he had missed the opportunity of a free communication on the critical situation "as respects the present state of the world, & our relations with the acting parties in it, in Europe, & in this hemisphere," and questioned pertinently whether "we can, in any form, take a bolder attitude regarding it, in favor of liberty. . . ." Jefferson's reply is noteworthy: "I have ever deemed it fundamental for the United States," he wrote,

never to take active part in the quarrels of Europe. Their political interests are entirely distinct from ours. Their mutual jealousies, their balance of power, their complicated alliances, their forms and principles of government, are all foreign to us. . . . On our part, never had a people so favorable a chance of trying the opposite system, of peace and fraternity with mankind. . . .

Later in 1823, Canning, the British foreign secretary, anxious to associate the government of the United States with that of Great Britain in a joint declaration against European interference in the question of the Spanish colonies, opened conversation with Richard Rush . . . Having no authority to accept Canning's proposals, Rush sent the dispatches to Monroe, who received them on October 9, just as he was on the point of leaving for Oakwood, his Virginia home. Adams, the secretary of state, had gone away to Quincy, and hence President Monroe turned naturally to Jefferson, to whom he sent the correspondence, along with a letter of his own, requesting him to submit it to Madison, and asking an opinion from each. "The project aims," he wrote,

in the first instance, at a mere expression of opinion, somewhat in the abstract. . . . My own impression is that we ought to meet the proposal of the British government, and to make known that we would view an interference on the part of the European powers, and especially an attack on the [Spanish-American] colonies by them, as an attack on ourselves.

In view of the importance of Jefferson's letter of October 24, which was evoked by this request, it is desirable to analyze it in some detail. Its prime significance lies in its creative suggestion of a permanent system of American foreign policy, with principles so broad as to be capable of wide application to new cases, not thought of at the time, and not limited to the immediate issues presented by the Canning overtures. Jefferson assured Monroe that the question presented by the Canning correspond-ence was the "most momentous . . . since that of independence," and that the circumstances produced by it were "auspicious" for the introduction and establishment of *the* American system, whose principles he had elaborated in intimate contact with him since his proposal of such a system three years earlier. Jefferson's letter contained, further, a clear-cut delineation of this American system, just as it had been predicted by Pradt, with the United States assuming the leadership, and with two definite principles: an exclusion of all European influence from the new world and an abstention from all participation in the affairs of the old world. . . .

Aside from the principle of non-colonization, which grew out of the specific contingency created by the Russian and British territorial claims to the northwest coast of America, Adams failed completely to suggest an enunciation of an American system of policy in the annual presidential message. Neither the draft of minutes made by Adams on November 13 nor the sketch of it made by Monroe contain any reference to any such declaration, nor do they contain the cardinal tenets of non-participation in European affairs and European non-participation in American affairs. The *Memoirs* of Adams likewise contain no intimation of his desire to see a public pronouncement such as Monroe actually made. . . .

For the separate statement of an American system of policy in the latter part of the presidential message, which came up for cabinet discussion after the British invitation to a joint declaration had become a closed incident, Jefferson must

receive chief credit. In his letter of advice, Jefferson specifically urged that the declaration of policy be brought to the attention of congress in the presidential message. As a consequence, Monroe, after having presented the paragraphs dealing with the matters suggested by Adams's draft of minutes in the cabinet meeting of November 21, read two additional paragraphs, which contained the first sketches of the Monroe Doctrine *per se*. . . . The paragraph which contained the two principles related to the doctrine of two spheres was largely an elaboration of Jefferson's letter of October 24. The impress of this letter upon Monroe's paragraph is unmistakable.

The fundamental maxim, Jefferson insisted, was "never to entangle ourselves in the broils of Europe." Monroe restated it in his message thus: "In the wars of the European powers in matters relating to themselves we have never taken any part, nor does it comport with our policy so to do."

The supplementary principle, Jefferson stated, was "never to suffer Europe to intermeddle with cis-Atlantic affairs," insisting that "America, North and South, has a set of interests of her own," that "she should therefore have a system of her own," and that the United States "will oppose, with all our means, the forcible interposition of any other power, as auxiliary, stipendiary, or under any other form or pretext, and most especially their transfer to any other power by conquest, cession, or acquisition in any other way." Monroe elaborated it thus:

The political system of the allied powers is essentially different . . . from that of America. . . . We should consider any attempt on their part to extend their system to any portion of this hemisphere as dangerous to our peace and safety. With the existing colonies or dependencies of any European power we have not interfered and shall not interfere. But with the Governments who have declared their independence . . . , we could not view any interposition for the purpose of oppressing them, or controlling in any other manner their destiny, by any European power, in any other light than as the manifestation of an unfriendly disposition toward the United States.

Moreover, there is conclusive evidence as to who influenced the president in drawing up his paragraph in regard to South America, in connection with which he stated the doctrine of two spheres, in the form of a letter written by Monroe to Jefferson on December 4th, which accompanied the copy of the presidential message. Monroe wrote:

I have concurr'd thoroughly with the sentiments express'd in your late letter, as I am persuaded, you will find, by the message, as to the part we ought to act, toward the allied powers, in regard to S. America. I consider the cause of that country, as essentially our own.

. . . Adams should not be given credit for the doctrine of two spheres as found in the latter part of Monroe's message. . . .

Though statements made by Adams both before and after the president informed him of his intention of enunciating an American policy in his annual message reflect the narrow and doctrinaire conception of the system he "earnestly recommended for this emergency," there are, nevertheless, evidences which might indicate that he envisaged something more than a mere exposition of republican principles. It might be pointed out that passages recorded by Adams in his *Memoirs* after the cabinet meeting of November 21 bear a remarkable similarity both in their language

and intent to the doctrine of two spheres as found in Monroe's address of December 2. However, by November 21, Adams had already read Jefferson's "decisively pronounced" delineation of the doctrine, which was submitted to him by Monroe six days previously, and on November 21 he heard the president's sketches of his message, which may have contained an enunciation of the doctrine. Hence, the principles he entered in his *Memoirs* on that day cannot be accepted unquestioningly as his own. Further, the president's paragraph containing the fundamental doctrine of the message was drawn up in its completed form by November 24, as has been shown, thus antedating the most important of the diplomatic drafts penned by Adams in reply to the British and Russian governments and also the most significant of his entries in his *Memoirs*. His communication of November 27 to the Russian government and his dispatch of November 30 to Rush, both of which were built upon the president's paragraph, furnished the basis upon which his claims to the authorship of the doctrine of two spheres in the message have rested and must largely rest.

For the momentous declaration of 1823, which forms the cornerstone of American foreign policy, a greater measure of credit must, therefore, be accorded the white-haired sage of Monticello. In his intimacy with his neighbor at Oakwood, he developed the American system, first impressing upon the president the importance of its adoption in 1820, asserting that it would be a "leading principle" with him had he longer to live, and finding in Canning's overtures three years later the "auspicious" circumstances in which "to introduce and establish" it.

WILLIAM A. MacCORKLE (1857–1930) was born in Virginia and educated in law at Washington and Lee. He moved to West Virginia, practiced law, entered politics, and was elected governor. His chief interest, however, was writing history and he produced books on Haiti, Nicaragua, and the Monroe Doctrine. In the selection that follows, he makes a case for Monroe's authorship based on an examination of the President's correspondence with Jefferson and Madison. There, he claims, may be found all the ideas that went into the Doctrine. They were Monroe's alone and he needed no assistance from his advisers except as sounding boards. Does the fact that Monroe stated the ideas of the Doctrine in letters preclude his having got them from someone else? Does it mean they were necessarily his?*

Conception and Enunciation Due to Monroe

During the summer and fall of 1823 Mr. Monroe and Mr. Adams were absent from Washington. During his vacation the President was wrestling with the question of the Spanish colonies. It was the one great question that was confronting his administration.

In the early summer of 1823, two or three months before the conferences on the enunciation of the doctrine, which took place in Washington before the cabinet, President Monroe wrote Mr. Jefferson:

WASHINGTON, June, 2, 1823.
Dear Sir,—I regretted very much that my duties here, with the necessity I was under to pass through London and remain there some days, detain'd me so long, as to deprive me of the pleasure of seeing you, on my late visit to Albemarle. Being informed by Mrs. Randolph that you intended to return in a fortnight, I should have prolong'd my stay there for that term, but was compelled to return, to receive the instructions, which had been prepared, for our ministers, who were just about to sail for Spain & So. America, & by other duties. The moment is peculiarly critical, as respects the present state of the world, & our relations with the acting parties in it, in Europe, & in this hemisphere, & it would have been very gratifying to me, to have had an opportunity of free communication with you, on all the interesting subjects connected with it. The French armies

---

* From William A. MacCorkle, *The Personal Genesis of the Monroe Doctrine*, pp. 62–87. New York: G. P. Putnam's Sons, 1923.

have enter'd Spain, and thus the Bourbon family have put at issue, by an offensive movement, its own fortune, perhaps its existence, for should the attack fail, they will have no claim, on the justice, if on the liberality, of any portion of those, even in France, at whose vital interests the blow was aim'd. What the precise organization, of the revolutionary force in Spain, is, or whether any is formed in France, are facts with which we have little knowledge. We cannot believe that the revolutionary spirit has become extinct in the latter country, after the astonishing feats perform'd in favor of liberty, by Frenchmen in latter days, nor can we suppose, that the governing power in Spain would have risk'd so much, or could have gone so far, had it not relied on the support of the nation. The British Govt. is, I fear, playing, rather into the hands of France & of the holy Alliance, so far at least, as to promote the establishment of a house of peers, in Spain, after its own model, than of affording to Spain the aid, which is so necessary to her independence, and to all just principles, at the present time. The motive is obvious. The court is, I have no doubt, in principle, with the holy Alliance, and is therefore averse, to aid Spain, in any manner, whereby to aid the cause of human rights. How far it may be driven from its policy, by the sentiments of the nation, is uncertain. We saw that in the struggle of France, G. Britain was the most decisive & active party against that cause. I think that a change has since been wrought, by many causes, but can form no estimate of the extent to which that change has gone. Russia looks, as is presumed, with peculiar anxiety to Constantinople, & so firmly is despotism establish'd there, that the Emperor, takes less interest, than the powers nearer at hand in what passes in the west & south of Europe. . . . Such is the state of Europe, & our relation to it is pretty much the same, as it was, in the commencement of the French revolution. Can we, in any form, take a bolder attitude in regard to it, in favor of liberty, than we then did? Can we afford greater aid to that cause, by assuming any

such attitude, than we now do, by the form of our example? These are subjects on which I should be glad to have your sentiments.

In regard to So. America our relations are very friendly, tho' the destiny of many of its parts, uncertain. The presumption is that the whole country will settle down under a republican system; but so great is the ignorance of the people & so little is the dependence to be plac'd on their popular leaders, that we cannot pronounce with certainty on the result. . . .   James Monroe.

The letter, not published by Mr. Ford in his statement and written more than two months before Canning's letter, rings like sharp steel and shows the writer's grasp of the situation and his determination to preserve the liberties of South America and to hold firmly in hand the attitude of his country as to this continent. Can any position be bolder? Is there any evidence in this letter of weakening in his long understood position of freedom and independence for the Americas? A reading of the letter will show that this subject, the premonition of the doctrine in his message, was the one nearest his heart. This was before any consultation with Mr. Adams.

When he received the dispatches from Minister Rush he took them with him on his vacation for study and reflection. On October 17th, two weeks before the return to Washington, and before there was any opportunity to discuss the question with his cabinet, he wrote again to Mr. Jefferson, stating the designs of the Holy Alliance against the independence of South America, and practically formulating the Monroe Doctrine.

Oakhill, October 17th, 1823.
Dear Sir,—I transmit to you two despatches, which were receiv'd from Mr. Rush, while I was lately in Washington, which in-

volve interests of the highest importance. They contain two letters from Mr. Canning, suggesting designs of the holy alliance, against the Independence of So. America, & proposing a co-operation, between G. Britain & the U. States, in support of it, against the members of that alliance. The project aims in the first instance, at a mere expression of opinion, somewhat in the abstract, but which it is expected by Mr. Canning, will have a great political effect, by defeating the combination. By Mr. Rush's answers, which are also enclosed, you will see the light in which he views the subject, & the extent to which he may have gone. Many important considerations are involved in this proposition. 1st. Shall we entangle ourselves, at all, in European politicks, & wars, on the side of any power, against others, presuming that a concert by agreemen, of the kind proposed, may lead to that result? 2d. If a case can exist, in which a sound maxim may, & ought to be departed from, is not the present instance, precisely that case? 3d. Has not the epoch arriv'd when G. Britain must take her stand, either on the side of the side of the monarchs of Europe, or of the U. States, & in consequence, either in favor of Despotism or of liberty & may it not be presum'd, that aware of that necessity, her government, has seig'd on the present occurrence, as that, which it deems, the most suitable, they announce & mark the commenc'ment of that career.

My own impression is that we ought to meet the proposal of the British govt., to make it known, that we would view an interference on the part of the European powers, and especially an attack on the Colonies, by them, as an attack on ourselves, presuming that if they succeeded with them, they would extend it to us.[1] I am sensible however of the extent, & difficulty of the question, & shall be happy to have yours, & Mr. Madison's opinions on it. I do not wish to trouble either of you with small objects, *but the present one is vital, involving the high interests, for which we have so long & so faithfully, & harmoniously contended to-*

gether.[1] Be so kind as to enclose to him the despatches, with an intimation of the motive. With great respect &c,

Recd Oct. 23.   James Monroe.

The three propositions are to be noted. Monroe asserts his own ideas as to the necessity for vigorous action on the part of this government, asks the opinion of his great advisors upon three important questions, and brings the question clean and clear as to the proposition of liberty and freedom on the side of America, as against interference on this continent on the part of monarchial Europe. . . .

This showed his own views before any consultation with his cabinet and especially with Mr. Adams, and was written to the two men to whom he was nearest and whose advice during a long lifetime he had considered of the highest value. On October 24th, Thomas Jefferson replied to this letter . . .

Monticello, October 24, 1823.
Dear Sir: The question presented by the letters you have sent me, is the most momentous which has ever been offered to my contemplation since that of Independence. That made us a nation, this sets our compass and points the course which we are to steer through the ocean of time opening on us. And never could we embark on it under circumstances more auspicious. Our first and fundamental maxim should be, never to entangle ourselves in the broils of Europe. *Our second, never to suffer Europe to intermeddle wtih cis-Atlantic affairs. America, North and South, has a set of interests distinct from those of Europe, and peculiarly her own. She should therefore have a system of her own, separate and apart from that of Europe.*[2] While the last is laboring to become the domicile of despotism, our endeavor should surely be, to make our hemisphere that of freedom. One nation, most of all, could disturb us in this pursuit; she now offers to lead, aid, and accompany us in it.

[1] Italics are MacCorkle's.—*Ed.*

[2] Italics are MacCorkle's.—*Ed.*

By acceding to her proposition, we detach her from the bands, bring her mighty weight into the scale of free-government, and emancipate a continent at one stroke, which might otherwise linger long in doubt and difficulty. Great Britain is the nation which can do us the most harm of any one, or all on earth; and with her on our side we need not fear the whole world. With her then, we should most sedulously cherish a cordial friendship; and nothing would tend more to knit our affections than to be fighting once more, side by side, in the same cause. Not that I would purchase even her amity at the price of taking part in her wars. But the war in which the present proposition might engage us, should that be its consequence, is not her war, but ours. Its object is to introduce and establish the American system, of keeping out of our land all foreign powers, of never permitting those of Europe to intermeddle with the affairs of our nations. It is to maintain our own principle, not to depart from it. And if, to facilitate this, we can effect a division in the body of the European powers, and draw over to our side its most powerful member surely we should do it. But I am clearly of Mr. Canning's opinion, that it will prevent instead of provoking war. With Great Britain withdrawn from their scale and shifted into that of our two continents, all Europe combined would not undertake such a war. For how would they propose to get at either enemy without superior fleets? Nor is the occasion to be slighted which this proposition offers, of declaring our protest against the atrocious violations of the rights of nations, by the interference of any one in the internal affairs of another, so flagitiously begun by Bonaparte, and now continued by the equally lawless Alliance, calling itself Holy. . . .

I should think it, therefore, advisable, that the Executive should encourage the British government to a continuance in the dispositions expressed in these letters, by an assurance of his concurrence with them as far as his authority goes; and that as it may lead to war, the declaration of which requires an act of Congress, the case shall be laid before them for consideration at their first meeting, and under the reasonable aspect in which it is seen by himself."

I have been so long weaned from political subjects, and have so long ceased to take any interest in them, that I am sensible I am not qualified to offer opinions on them worthy of any attention. But the question now proposed involves consequences so lasting, and effects so decisive of our future destinies, as to rekindle all the interest I have heretofore felt on such occasions, and to induce to the hazard of opinions, which will prove only my wish to contribute still my mite towards anything which may be useful to our country. And praying you to accept it at only what it is worth, I add the assurance of my constant and affectionate friendship and respect.

Th. Jefferson.

Mr. Madison's letter expresses similar views of the subject:

Montpellier, Oct. 30, 1823.
Dear Sir:—I have recd from Mr. Jefferson your letter to him, with the correspondence between Mr. Canning and Mr. Rush, sent for his and my perusal, and our opinions on the subject of it.

From the disclosures of Mr. Canning it appears as was otherwise to be inferred, that the success of France against Spain would be followed by attempts of the Holy Alliance to reduce the revolutionized colonies of the latter to their former dependence.

The professions we have made to these neighbors, our sympathy with their Liberties & Independence, the deep interests we have in the most friendly relations with them, and the consequences threatened by a command of their resources by the great powers confederated against the Rights & Reforms of which we have given so conspicuous & persuasive an example, all unite in calling for our efforts to defeat the meditated crusade. It is particularly fortunate that the policy of G. Britain tho' guided by calculations different from ours, has presented a cooperation for an object the same with ours. With that cooperation we have nothing to fear from the rest of Europe; and with it the best reliance on success to our just & laudible views. There ought not to be any backwardness therefore, I think, in meeting her in the way she has proposed; keeping in view of course the spirit and forms of the Constitution in every step taken in the road to war which must be the last step, if those short of war should be without avail.

It cannot be doubted that Mr. Canning's proposal tho' made with the air of *consultation*[3] as well as concert, was founded on predetermination to take the course marked out whatever might be the reception given here to his invitation. But this consideration ought not to divert us from what is just and proper in itself. Our co-operation is due to ourselves & to the world; and whilst it must ensure success in the event of an appeal to force, it doubles the chance of success without that appeal. It is not improbable that G B would like best to have the sole merit of being the Champion of her new friends notwithstanding the greater difficulty to be encountered, but for the dilemma in which she would be placed. She must in that case either leave us as neutral to extend our commerce & navigation at the expense of hers, or to make us Enemies by renewing her paper blockades, and other arbitrary proceedings on the Ocean. It may be hoped that such a dilemma will not be without a permanent tendency to check her proneness to unnecessary wars.

Why the British Cabinet should have scrupled to arrest the calamity it now apprehends, by applying to the threats of France agst Spain the "small effort" which it scruples not to employ on behalf of Spanish America, is best known to itself. It is difficult to find any other explanation than that *interest* in the one case has more weight in her casuistry than principle had in the other.

Will it not be honorable to our country & possibly not altogether in vain to invite

[3] Italics are Madison's.—*Ed.*

the British Govt to extend the avowed disapprobation of the project agst the Spanish Colonies, to the enterprize of France agst Spain herself; and even to join in some declaratory act in behalf of the Greeks? On the supposition that no form could be given to the act of clearing it of a pledge to follow it up by war, we ought to compare the good to be done, with the little injury to be apprehended to the U. S. shielded as their interests would be by the power & the fleets of G. Britain united with their own. These are questions however which may require more information than I possess, and more reflection than I can now give them.

What is the extent of Mr. Canning's disclaimer to "the remaining possessions of Spain in America?" Does it exclude future views of acquiring Porto-Rico &c. as well as Cuba? It leaves G. B. free as I understand it, in relations to Spanish possessions in other Quarters of the Globe.

I return the correspondence of Mr. R. & Mr. C. with assurances of the highest respect & sincerest regard.

James Madison.

To prove that James Monroe did not comprehend the significance of his action when he announced the Monroe Doctrine, with its principles that America should be for Americans ringing in his ears, in a direct reply to his request for advice made by him to the greatest living American statesmen, appears to be hard task. In view of this great interest on the part of Mr. Monroe, and the direct advice from his two most trusted counselors, is it not somewhat unreasonable to say that, however vigorous and earnest was Mr. Adams, it was through his action that the President was induced to announce the doctrine, or that the theory was conceived and the principle carried to its fruition practically by Mr. Adams? The President's mind was made up, as is clearly shown above, long before Mr. Adams returned to Washington.

On November 7th the first cabinet meeting was had after the summer vacation. The question arose on the letters of Mr. Rush and Mr. Canning, and the answer to the Russian minister. The President, so far from evincing any timidity, or showing any wavering of his determination to preserve the prestige of America, in the language of Mr. Adams, "was averse to any course which should have the position of taking any position subordinate to that of Great Britain, and suggested the idea of sending a special minister to *protest* against the interposition of the Holy Alliance." And again, at the same meeting, "The President referring to instructions given before the Congress of Aix-la-Chapelle, declaring that we would, if invited, attend no meeting relative to South America of which less than its entire independence should be the object intimated that similar limitations might be assumed now."

The preparation of the message was by reports by heads of departments, which were considered in full meetings of the cabinet. The long series of meetings between November 7th and the 2nd of December show that the subject of the American colonies was gone over in every possible shape and detail by all of the members of the cabinet. This cabinet was composed of William H. Crawford, Samuel Lewis Southard, John C. Calhoun, William Wirt, and John Quincy Adams; and throughout the long days of these discussions one proposition absolutely clearly appears: That James Monroe was emphatically the head of the administration and that while he was vigorous and determined to preserve the freedom of this hemisphere from the control of Europe, he was endeavoring,

if possible, to preserve the peace of the world.

Mr. Adams says that, "he was alarmed beyond anything that he could have conceived with the fear that the Holy Alliance was about to restore all of South America to Spain."

He surely had room for alarm, because a great portion of his life had been spent either directly in the horrors of war or among the resulting effects of conflict. It was his administration, of which he was the responsible head, which had to embark in the conflict if there should be one.

In no sense of the word, by this discussion, do we wish to say anything to lessen the great credit which in these days should cling around the life of John Quincy Adams. He was a great patriot, a distinguished diplomat,—honest, able, sincere, and as determined for freedom as any one that lived in that day and time. . . .

On the 21st the President read the sketch which he had prepared for his message, and instead of its showing any timidity or fear, [it] . . . "sounded an alarm of war like a thunder clap."

Mr. Adams endeavored to persuade him to subdue the vigor of his statement, because he feared that a statement so pointed might cause the war which they were trying to avert. Through the discussions of the cabinet, in which Mr. Adams bore a most vigorous part, the President modified the statement and within a few days it was read to the cabinet and agreed to by Mr. Adams, being drawn up in the spirit which he had urged on the former day. Mr. Adams expressly says:

In the discussion of the letter to be directed to Baron Tuyl[1], the paper itself was drawn to correspond exactly with the paragraph of the President's message which he had read to me yesterday and which was entirely conformable to the system of policy which I have earnestly recommended for this emergency.

Throughout the discussion before the cabinet there was much contention over the proposition as to how the statement of the position of the United States should be announced: whether in connection with Great Britain, as an independent statement, or as a communication by the Secretary of State to the foreign ministers. The contention is that it was through Mr. Adams that the announcement was made to the world by a message to Congress.

A fair statement of the position of Mr. Monroe as to this is contained in his amendment to the letter to Mr. Rush, and in his letter to Mr. Jefferson after the message had been delivered. It is here noted that Mr. Adams, in all the discussions in and about this period and about all these matters, possesses a great advantage because of his daily Diary, which is extant, and easily obtainable. It is practically the only detailed statement dealing with the intimate discussions of the cabinet, excepting the letters of the parties thereto. Mr. Adams was a man who believed in himself to a greater extent than he did in any one else, and while no one doubts the honesty of his statements, they all must be taken with that question of self-importance which lingers around every man's account of his own life and actions.

Naturally Mr. Adams's Diary and Memoirs so accessible would be the mine in which people would delve for information concerning the intimate political transactions covering that event. With the exception of Mr. Monroe's letters there is no written document emanating

from him explaining his share in this transaction. What we have from him are his letters, and the further and conclusive proposition more important than any other is that as President of the United States he announced the Monroe Doctrine; that he was the head of the Government which promulgated this great doctrine, and not only was he the titular head but he was the active controlling dominating power in his Administration, and that he himself was replete with more political experience than any other man of his day and generation. . . .

Mr. Monroe's letters and writings have now been collected, and his memory is beginning to feel the advantage of this work; for heretofore there was but little, except his public messages, accessible to the scholar who was attempting to get a history of the events which touched the mainsprings of his lifetime in the discussions of the cabinet. Mr. Monroe's letter to Thomas Jefferson, written after the message was announced, shows what he had done, and the principles which had animated him in the enunciation of the doctrine.

Washington, Decr. 4, 1823.
Dear Sir,—I now forward to you a copy of the message, more legible than that which (was) sent by the last mail. *I have concurr'd thoroughly with the sentiments expressed in your late letter, as I am persuaded, you will find, by the message, as to the part we ought to act, toward the allied powers, in regard to So. America. I consider the cause of that country as essentially our own.*[4] That the crisis is fully as menacing, as has been supposed, is confirmed, by recent communications, from another quarter, with which I will make you acquainted in my next. . . .
Rec'd Dec. 7.   James Monroe.

[4] Italics are MacCorkle's.—*Ed.*

You will observe that he says, "I have concurred thoroughly with the sentiments expressed in your late letter, as I am persuaded, you will find, by the message, as to the part we ought to act, toward the allied powers, in regard to South America. I consider the cause of that country as essentially our own." Does this statement show that this great President was holding a trumpet for his subordinate to blow?

In his second letter, of December, 1823, after the letter of the 4th, he specifically discusses the details of the transaction in which our government had taken its own initiative, separate from Great Britain, thus giving our position greater strength with allied Europe, and the letter gives specifically his own views of the occurrences leading to the method of communication, to the world.

Washington, Decr. 1823.

Dear Sir,—Shortly after the receipt of yours of the 24th of October, & while the subject treated in it, was under consideration, the Russian minister, drew the attention of the govt. to the same subject, tho' in a very different sense from that which it had been done by Mr. Canning. Baron Tuyll, announced in an official letter and as was understood by order of the Emperor, that having heard that the republic of Columbia had appointed a minister to Russia, he wished it to be distinctly understood that he would not receive him, nor would he receive any minister from any of the new govts, de facto, of which the new world had been recently the theatre. On another occasion, he observ'd, that the Emperor had seen with great satisfaction, the declaration of this govt., when those new govts. were recognized, that it was the intention of the U States, to remain neutral. He gave this intimation for the purpose of expressing the wish of his master, that we would persevere in the same policy. He communicated soon afterwards, an extract of a letter from his govt, in which the conduct of the allied powers, in regard to Naples, Spain & Portugal, was reviewed, and that policy explain'd, distinctly avowing their determination, to crush all revolutionary movements, & thereby to preserve order in the civilized world. . . .

When the character of these communications, of that from Mr. Canning & that from the Russian minister, is considered, & the time when made, it leaves little doubt that some project against the new govts., is contemplated. In what form is uncertain. It is hoped that the sentiments expressed in the message, will give a check to it. We certainly meet, in full extent, the proposition of Mr. Canning, & in the mode to give it greatest effect. If his govt. makes a similar decln., the project will, it may be presumed, be abandoned. By taking the step here, it is done in a manner more conciliatory with, & respectful to Russia, & the other powers, than if taken in England, and as it is thought with more credit to our govt. Had we moved in the first instance in England, separated as she is in part, from those powers, our union with her, being marked, might have produced irritation with them. We know that Russia dreads a connection between the U States and G. Britain, or harmony in policy. Moving on our own ground, the apprehension that unless she retreats, that effect may be produced, may be a motive with her for retreating. Had we mov'd in England, it is probable, that it would have been inferr'd that we acted under her influence, & at her instigation, & thus have lost credit as well with our southern neighbours, as with the allied powers. . . .

Very sincerely your friend

recd Dec. 11.   (no signature)

This letter shows . . . that "the masterstroke at this junction, of warning off European aggressiveness in an opening message to Congress, rather than by a joint protest with England was Monroe's own idea."

WILLIAM W. KAUFMANN (1918–   ) sees the
wellsprings of George Canning's overtures in the
balance of power. The United States was important
as an ally to help in denouncing the plans of the
Continental powers to invade South America.
Kaufmann's focus is on the international relations
of the great powers.*

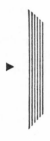

American Diplomatic
Support Sought

[In 1822, while the Duke of Wellington, British representative at Verona, was
opposing the policies of the Continental
powers,] Canning busied himself with
preparations for the recognition of the
Latin American states. In his own mind
there was no need to justify such an act;
it was obviously a requirement of the
national interest. The chief difficulty facing him was that of making recognition
palatable both to his colleagues and to
Europe. The majority of Lord Liverpool's[1] cabinet, veterans in one way or
another of the Napoleonic Wars, held
revolution in as great abhorrence as did
the Tsar. They had looked in another

[1] British prime minister.—Ed.

direction as long as Castlereagh directed
affairs; he, after all, had been a gentle-
man and an aristocrat. But this new man
with the flowing eloquence and the sear-
ing wit was something quite different.
Whatever he proposed must undergo
their most critical scrutiny. Canning
understood that he would need all his
ingenuity and eloquence to circumvent
them.

As for the Continental Powers, it was
not precisely their approval that he
sought. Rather was it their immobility
—the immobility, let us say, that would
result from the collapse of the Concert.
And their inability at some later date
to use his action as a precedent for

* From William W. Kaufmann, *British Policy and Latin America*, pp. 142–153. Reprinted
without footnotes by permission of Yale University Press. Copyright 1951 by Yale University Press.

policies in Europe inimical to English interests. In other words he must base his recognition upon grounds difficult even for the Continental Powers to gainsay, and he must declare himself at a moment when their talent for cooperative retaliation had become exhausted. The first and most obvious step in such a game was to demonstrate—as Castlereagh had so frequently demonstrated—the impossibility of bringing Spain to reason.

In September Canning began methodically to complain of the sporadic Spanish interference with the Latin American trade of Great Britain. In October he remarked ominously

that if England forebore to prejudge the question of a possible amicable settlement between Spain and her ancient Colonies . . . she did so, in the complete understanding and on the condition distinctly admitted by Spain, that her trade with those Colonies should be free and unmolested . . .

In November he announced in a reasoned memorandum to the cabinet that since Spain was no longer carrying out her share of the bargain (which, if it ever existed, had never been reduced· to writing), he must dispatch a naval expedition to the Caribbean to prevent further attacks upon British commerce. That such an expedition must cooperate with the insurgent authorities in Latin America to accomplish its purpose, that such cooperation must lead in turn to some sort of understanding with them—these things he hardly doubted. That the entire maneuver might result in the establishment of regular diplomatic relations—this he did not say; but what fruits might the future not yield?

To protect himself from the accusation of traveling too fast, to exhibit his extraordinary patience, Canning at the same time took another and even more familiar step. On November 30, 1822, he offered Spain the services of Great Britain as mediator in the Latin American dispute. He went on, having made this pleasant and meaningless gesture, to deny to France and the United States that he harbored territorial designs upon any of the colonies. In the privacy of the Foreign Office he also drew up a list of the consuls to be sent to Latin America. The stage was being set, and events in Europe were rapidly approaching the ripe state of confusion which Canning needed in order to act.

French policy during December left the impression that the final scene might be played even sooner than Canning had anticipated. When Wellington reached Paris from Verona he found Villèle[2] apparently bent upon avoiding intervention in Spain. To all intents and purposes the rump Alliance was collapsing under the weight of British displeasure and its own internal discords. Canning seized upon the occasion and offered to mediate between France and Spain—no doubt hoping to evoke further evidences of disunity by this gesture. The move, much disliked by Wellington, appeared to have its effect. While Russia, Prussia, and Austria signed a circular dispatch announcing their intention to withdraw their envoys from Spain, France held back. The Duc de Montmorency rejected Canning's offer of mediation on December 24—but on the plausible ground that the differences between France and Spain were not sufficiently serious to warrant British intervention. And on the following day this most powerful advocate of collaboration with the Alliance resigned as Minister of Foreign Affairs, to be replaced by the exuberant Chateaubriand. At the same time the Spanish government learned that the French

[2] French prime minister.—*Ed.*

ambassador in Madrid would not be withdrawn. Here, indeed, was confusion twice confounded.

As the currents of European politics became more disorderly Canning happily turned his attention back to Spain. "Let Spain do us justice fully and handsomely" in Latin America, he explained, "and so enable us to behave towards her with that singleness of conduct" as her protector in Europe "which is as much our desire, as it is her interest, that we should pursue." The Spanish government, terrified by the multitude of pressures, had already entered into negotiations with the colonists for the recognition of their independence. It now became even more pliant, promising to withdraw all restrictions against trading with Latin America and give satisfaction for those English ships which had been captured while engaged in the trade. Confronted with this extraordinary *volte-face,* Canning found it necessary to suspend his decision to send out consuls.

But were these Spanish gestures sincere or brought on merely by the European crisis? Would Spain, moreover, make it clear to Latin America that Great Britain had inspired them? This last point was particularly important; and so there went off to Sir William A'Court, the British minister at Madrid, a singular dispatch. If the Spaniards misconstrue us, Canning wrote,

if they evince mistrust instead of thankfulness, and deny to us the means of satisfying England upon points of English interest; they may depend upon it, that the sins of American Spain will not only enable but compel us to remain not only neutral, but indifferent to the fate of Spain in Europe.

In other words it was no longer enough for Spain to accept the inevitable; she must acknowledge the assistance afforded by Great Britain in removing the scales from her eyes. Otherwise—the threat was clearly implied—Canning would recognize the independence of the colonies without further reference to her feelings.

That Canning already felt free to do so without further reference to Europe goes almost without saying. He knew surely that no single Power could stop him; and the Alliance, in its disordered state, how could it retaliate? It was, he assured his ambassador in St. Petersburg, split "into three parts as distinct as the constitutions of England, France, and Muscovy." The shabby business of subordinating British interests to its whims had ended. Villèle, he announced happily, was a minister of thirty years ago—

no revolutionary scoundrel: but constitutionally hating England, as Choiseul and Vergennes used to hate us—and so things are getting back to a wholesome state again. Every nation for itself, and God for us all. Only bid your Emperor [Alexander] be quiet, for the time for Areopagus, and the like of that, is gone by.

Yet as the new year dawned Canning's conviction somehow failed to be borne out by the facts. Spain, to be sure, remained submissive, her liberal government humbly willing to do his bidding. But France suddenly commenced to lend a half-hearted allegiance to the Alliance, while the Eastern Powers, faced with the secession of Great Britain, struggled bravely to maintain an unbroken front. Faithful to the Verona agreements, Prussia withdrew her ambassador from Madrid on January 9, 1823. The following day Austria and Russia did likewise. On January 18, after a decent interlude of silence, Chateaubriand ordered the French envoy to join the diplomatic exodus.

From Canning's point of view the parade of ambassadors was ominous enough; but there was worse yet to follow. On January 28 Louis XVIII in a speech from the throne announced that the situation in Madrid had become intolerable. Unless Ferdinand the Well-beloved were set free "to give to his people the institutions they cannot hold but from him," French troops would march to his rescue.

Instead of finding confusion and paralysis, Canning beheld the shocking, the incredible, spectacle of the rump Alliance, in apparent good order, bearing down upon Spain. Now was hardly the time to recognize colonies; he must first devote his energies to staving off this new expression of the Concert's will—French intervention. In January he pleaded with Chateaubriand: "Negotiate at least before you invade. Leave the Spanish revolution to burn itself out within its own crater; you have nothing to apprehend from the eruption, if you do not open a channel for the lava through the Pyrenees." In February he warned the Count d'Artois of the animosity aroused in England by the French King's speech. Pressing hard on the weak link of the Alliance he announced in the same month increases in Great Britain's naval strength. France continued her preparations to invade. Canning lifted the long-standing embargo upon the export of arms to Spain—and to Latin America. The Eastern Powers responded by assuring France of their support in the event that Great Britain should depart from her neutrality. By the middle of March the diplomatic contest had resolved itself in their favor. Canning could count upon only limited support from the country; the King and the cabinet had opposed him at every turn in the struggle.

It was an infuriating and frustrating experience. Canning's intelligence indicated that France was using the Alliance merely as a shield to ward off outside intervention, that her ambitions were purely French in scope. The manner in which she had delayed all her maneuvers, acting each time a step behind the Eastern Powers so as to flaunt her independence of them, certain expressions of the Count d'Artois and Villèle, the communications of Sir Charles Stuart—all these things confirmed him in the accuracy of his estimate. But here was the rub: he could muster no support for a firmer policy. The façade of the Alliance appeared too imposing, and a majority of the cabinet, abetted by the King, were actually wishing success to French arms. On March 21 he reluctantly confided to the French chargé d'affaires that Great Britain would be neutral in the impending conflict. Ten days later he announced the decision in an official memorandum. He could add only, and somewhat lamely, that England would take up arms were France to make her occupation of Spain permanent, were she to invade Portugal, or were she to try appropriating any part of the Spanish colonies. The final result was a sad climax to his earlier protestations about the disunity of Europe.

The French government welcomed Canning's statement, ignored his conditions, and proceeded with its plans. The Duc d'Angoulême had already left Paris for the frontier to assume command of the armies. On April 6, 1823, for the second time in two decades, French troops invaded Spain. Upon this occasion they met with only token resistance and the invasion quickly developed into a triumphal parade. In vain Austria, Russia, and Prussia sought to share in its direction. Although Villèle reluctantly agreed to the establishment of an Allied control council in Paris, its decisions had no effect upon the conduct of the war. The French armies simply advanced too swiftly. By May 24 they were in Madrid. On June 11, as they progressed southward, the harried Spanish government with Ferdinand in tow fled from Seville to Cadiz, there to make a last futile stand. To all intents and purposes the conflict was over; the power and glory of French arms had been vindicated. There remained only to liberate Ferdinand—an annoying but necessary task. It was for this purpose, after all, that the war had been fought.

In England Canning made the best of a most embarrassing situation. He was by turns boastful, defiant, and sarcastic. To an old friend he admitted that he had "had an itch for war with France, and that a little provocation might have scratched it into eruption; but fortunately the better reason prevailed, and I look back upon the decision with entire and perfect self-congratulation." On April 15 he appeared before the bar of the House of Commons and in a burst of calculated confidence unparalleled in the annals of English diplomacy read off a series of secret communications that had passed between Great Britain and the Alliance. The House wildly cheered the liberal sentiments which he had expressed. To the French chargé d'affaires he remarked sardonically: "Be yours the glory of victory followed by disaster and ruin, be ours the inglorious traffic of industry and an ever-increasing prosperity." The words of Burke rose to his lips: "The age of chivalry is gone; and an age of economists and calculators has succeeded." On April 30, 1823, he announced:

We determined that it was our duty, in the first instance, to endeavour to preserve peace, for all the world; next to endeavour

to preserve peace between the nations whose pacific relations appeared most particularly exposed to hazard; and, failing in this, to preserve at all events peace for this country.

The House of Commons rewarded these sentiments with an overwhelming vote of confidence—372 to 20; and Princess Lieven hastily explained to her brother that:

The English public is beginning to display a little common sense; what is more to the point, an appreciation of its own interest—the first consideration with the English. They will not spend a shilling on those interesting Spaniards, the objects of their good wishes.

What Princess Lieven failed to understand was that this vote of confidence, while expressing the peaceful inclinations of the country, also endowed Canning with new strength in dealing with his colleagues. The Tory majority was responding to his scintillations as Lord Liverpool had hoped it would; but in so doing it had sounded the death knell to the influence of that aged triumvirate, Lords Eldon, Sidmouth, and Westmoreland. Faced with the alternative of destroying the cabinet or acquiescing in the policies of the Foreign Secretary, they grudgingly chose to remain in office. Henceforward, despite their protests and delaying tactics, Canning was to become his own master in the realm of foreign affairs. He told Bagot quite bluntly that since April 30 and the vote of confidence "I have had pretty much my own way; and I believe you may now consider my politicks as those of the Government, as well as of the Country."

But what was he to do with this newfound freedom? The events of the three previous months had dealt a grievous blow to the prestige of Great Britain. The Alliance, so cavalierly defied at

Verona, had moved on majestically without her. Indeed, as Spanish resistance crumbled before the onslaughts of the French, the pretensions of its members seemed actually to increase. By April Canning was already hearing of their intention to find some way of restoring Ferdinand to his Latin American dominions. Was this the opportunity that he had thought to find in January and which had so quickly eluded him? Could it be possible that the Concert was at last preparing to assume a responsibility far beyond its physical capabilities? He could forestall the plot immediately, of course, simply by recognizing the Latin American states, as the United States had done a year earlier; but that would only drive the Continental Powers closer together. The wiser course seemed first to allow the Allies to overextend themselves —challenge them to do their worst—and then, having exposed their collective impotence to the world, defy them by the act of recognition. Surely, if the spectacle were staged with sufficient finesse, the Alliance would expire of mortification.

The scheme possessed only one notable defect: he could not operate all the levers alone. The Allies, led by France, having finished with Spain, would certainly attempt to determine the destinies of the revolutionists in Latin America; and, since this would be tantamount to a direct challenge to England, a passive attitude would just as certainly be impossible. Yet if Canning denounced the Allies by himself, they might ignore him even as they had in January, persist blindly in their plans, and bring about the very war that he wished to avoid. A denunciation, in order to be effective in this charged and uncertain atmosphere, must come with such éclat, with such an imposing show of force, that the Allies, convinced of its sincerity, would stop—

would in fact retreat from the scene in complete disorder. Such a denunciation plainly required at least the momentary support of another Power in order to lend that touch of conviction which Great Britain's actions alone would lack. For that support Canning turned to the United States.

The moment seemed highly propitious; after an interval of almost a year Adams himself was evincing a renewed interest in some sort of negotiation with Great Britain. He had, in fact, become aware of the growing differences between Canning and the Alliance and no doubt wished to profit from them by demanding a settlement of all issues left outstanding from the War of 1812. But Stratford Canning, the British minister in Washington, interpreted the Secretary's intentions in a broader and more optimistic sense. In March he reported upon the satisfaction with which Adams "viewed the course adopted by His Majesty's Cabinet in the present crisis of European Affairs . . ." In May he told Canning:

The course which you have taken in the great politics of Europe, has had the effect of making the English almost popular in the United States. The improved tone of public feeling is very perceptible, and even Adams has caught something of the soft infection. . . . On the whole, I question whether for a long time there has been so favorable an opportunity—as far as general disposition and good will are concerned,— to bring the two Countries nearer together.

Finally, on June 6, 1823, Stratford was able to write that

Instructions . . . are preparing for Mr. Rush . . . to negotiate a Convention with His Majesty's Government, principally on the subject of Slave Trade and Colonial Intercourse, but also with the view of conferring, and, if possible, of establishing a common understanding, on several points affecting the interests of the two Countries.

What more could Canning ask? He had already initiated certain steps of his own to prepare the American minister in London for such a rapprochement. Rush suddenly found himself subjected to toasts flattering to the principles of Jeffersonian neutrality, to dinner parties, charades, copies of parliamentary oratory, and other special attentions. But, as was only natural, Canning preferred to have the first overtures in this game originate in the United States. Whatever the bargain he had to strike in order to obtain American cooperation would thereby cost him the less. With a rare patience he waited and wrote up a series of instructions to guide a commission of inquiry to Mexico.

Rush did not receive his instructions from Adams until July 29. Then he waited for eighteen days, studying the topics of negotiation, before he requested an interview with Canning. The interlude must have been a painful one for the Foreign Secretary. The French were speeding toward Cadiz; Ferdinand would soon be free and the Allies at liberty to embark upon more elaborate schemes. The question of Latin America was already stirring in both Paris and Vienna. Clearly, if the United States was to be brought into the field against the Alliance, an agreement as to terms must be reached with some dispatch.

The tension finally eased when on August 16 Rush appeared at the Foreign Office. Almost inevitably, after certain preliminaries, the topic of Latin America came to the fore. Rush introduced the subject with the remark "that should France ultimately effect her purpose in Spain, there was at least the consolation left that Great Britain would not allow her to go farther and lay her hands upon the Spanish colonies, bringing them too under her grasp." Canning seized the opportunity with what must have been a barely concealed impatience and proceeded to elaborate his own ideas upon the matter. He immediately recommended Anglo-American cooperation as a remedy to the Continental menace. Not, he explained, "that any concert in action under it could become necessary between the two countries, but that the simple fact of our being known to hold the same sentiment would . . . by its moral effect, put down the intention on the part of France . . ."

A mixture of interest and suspicion constituted the reaction of the American minister. On the one hand, cooperation with Great Britain to protect the Latin American states from aggression, might, aside from its intrinsic value, serve as the preliminary to an agreement upon other outstanding issues. On the other hand, cooperation on this particular issue could cause his country infinite embarrassment. For the United States, having recognized the Latin American countries, would be bound in all good faith to honor its pledge; while Great Britain, having so far avoided the first obligation, would be free at any time to ignore the second. In an effort to avoid the dilemma Rush therefore urged Canning to bring Great Britain upon the common ground of recognition with the United States before entering into any cooperative enterprise.

But recognition was the last rather than the first step that Canning wished to take. His policy was intercontinental; his object was to destroy the Alliance; and the best way of accomplishing his purpose was to allow the Concert to try to intervene in Latin America. Premature acknowledgment of the new states might spoil the whole game.

GEORGE DANGERFIELD (1904–   ) was born in England but has lived in the United States since 1930 and is an American citizen. Educated at Oxford, he was a magazine editor before settling down in Santa Barbara to write history. His *Era of Good Feelings,* which won both the Bancroft and Pulitzer prizes, is a history of the Monroe administration. The section on diplomacy, from which the following selection is taken, relates the origin of Canning's overture to the United States to the rise of industrialism in Britain. Unlike Kaufmann, who searches for Canning's courtship of the United States in his concern for the balance of power, Dangerfield sees him as inviting the American consumer to provide the market for the increasing British manufactures.*

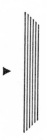

New Markets Needed

The year 1823 was in many larger and more dramatic respects a crucial year in the relations between the New World and the Old. It was the year when the conquerors of Napoleon came to a definite parting of the ways—the British constitutionalists moving towards the principle of nationalism (or competition) and the great reactionaries of Austria, Prussia, and Russia marching in a disorderly fashion towards the principle of Order (or monopoly). It was partly if not chiefly because of this immense disagreement in Europe that the United States was able to define its position in the world in the famous Message that has come down to us as the Monroe Doctrine. . . .

Canning's return to the Foreign Office [in 1822], a portentous event in European and American history, came at a time (even more portentous) when the British Industrial Revolution was well on the way to completing the middle stage of its development. The problem of the application of steam power to manufacture had almost been solved. The "Malleable Iron Period" was approaching the top of its climax in James B. Neilson's discovery of the use of hot air in smelting. The Age of Steam was

* From *The Era of Good Feelings* by George Dangerfield, copyright, 1952, by Harcourt, Brace & World, Inc., and reprinted with their permission. Pp. 274–275, 277–278, 280–289, 291–292.

in its dawn, but the age of horses and waterfalls and charcoal was manifestly passing away. The statistics of coal and iron production would tell the tale; but the most striking and eloquent version was provided by the cotton industry. The figures (which are of course very rough ones) show that in the period 1819 to 1821, for example, English mills spun 106,500,000 lbs. of cotton yarn, while in the period 1829 to 1831 they spun 216,500,000 lbs. Weaving was less progressive than spinning—the hand loom in 1830 still outnumbered the steam loom by more than four to one—but the cost of labor in the first period was said to be $15\frac{1}{2}d.$, and in the second only $9d.$ per pound of goods. The organization of the English factory system was, therefore, well on its way by 1830, though it still had a long distance to travel; and the relation between the growth of the English factory system and the rise of English liberalism is so obvious that we need hardly remind ourselves that the period 1918–21 coincided with the first Parliamentary clamor for free trade, and the period 1829 to 1831 with the great agitation for a middle-class Reform Bill.

There have always been spectacular, extraneous personages in the story of British industrialization. Besides the great names of early inventors, for example, we have to place those of Robert Clive and Warren Hastings, who looted the treasuries of Hindustan for the capital with which the great inventions were financed. And the middle stage of the British Industrial Revolution is inseparably connected with the name of George Canning. . . .

On April 14, 1823, George Canning made a great speech in Parliament which publicly reiterated the arguments he had already made to the French government in his dispatch of March 31. "I earnestly hope and trust," he declared in his peroration, "that she (constitutional Spain) may come triumphantly out of the struggle." His neutral policy was approved by the Commons, a mild victory for common sense, since England had no troops ready and her fleet could have been of no assistance to the Constitutionalists. But his hopes for the triumph of revolutionary Spain were dashed by the event; and his views were certainly not well received by the king or the Ultra members of the Cabinet. The Duke of Wellington had been obliged to say things at Verona which he did not altogether believe; and—what was worse—after he had said them they had been disregarded by the French and the Allies. His mortification took the form of an intrigue against Canning. Those who examine the letters of Madame de Lieven to Prince Metternich can watch it grow. It consisted of a series of attempts to humiliate Canning into resigning, and of a confidential correspondence between Metternich, Wellington, and George IV which was never shown to the Foreign Secretary. Canning was immovable. He knew that his policy was a popular one, he commanded a majority in the House of Commons, and above all he enjoyed the steady and unflinching support of the Earl of Liverpool.[1] . . .

Canning had hoped that the prestige of England would keep the French out of Spain, and that the Holy Allies would listen to his warnings and cease to meddle with the independence of Spanish America: his neutral policy was always directed towards the preservation of the Central and South American market. In the summer of 1823, it did not appear that

[1] British prime minister.

he had been successful. At his own dinner table, surrounded by Holy Alliance diplomats, George IV rallied his Foreign Secretary. "There is nothing more contemptible and clumsy than half-measures and half-tones. I hate them. *Don't you, Mr. Canning?*" Mr. Canning was silent. But, indeed, his diplomatic defeats were only on the surface. An instinct, too profound for formulation, urged him to shatter the Quadruple Alliance and to dissociate England from the Holy Allies. A British statesman, he said in 1826, "in internal as in external affairs [will] hold a middle course between extremes, avoiding alike extravagancies of despotism, or the licentiousness of unbridled freedom." Even in 1923, he was groping his way towards that kind of world liberalism which is most agreeable to an expanding industrial economy—the liberalism, that is to say, not of free men but of free markets. "With painful steps and slow" Lord Liverpool and his "economic Cabinet" were moving in the same direction. Needless to say, these pioneers did not reach their destination: they were not too sure—they could only hope—that it existed. While Lord Liverpool and Mr. Huskisson hacked away at the jungle of tariff schedules and navigation laws, Mr. Canning succeeded in discrediting the Holy Alliance. All loom together in British history as the heralds of a new era. . . .

When Mr. Canning began his battle with France and the Neo-Holy Allies, Great Britain was climbing out of her postwar depression. The fall in world prices, owing to a shortage of specie and an absence of an elastic credit system, did not hurt her industrial system with its exportable surplus. Her manufacturers were learning those technical refinements which reduce costs. As the collapse of the American cotton market had shown, raw materials were becoming cheap; and though wages are said not to have fallen as low as prices, the English industrial worker of those days was one of the most cruelly exploited people in the world. The British manufacturer, therefore, was able to quote prices that could attract even the misery of postwar Europe: but his chief single market was still the United States of America. As Lord Liverpool had told the House of Lords in 1820, whoever wished prosperity to England must wish prosperity to the United States. In 1822, 95 per cent of all its imports of woolen goods and 89 per cent of its imports of cotton goods were of British manufacture; in 1823, the percentages were 96 and 84. In 1822, 47 per cent of its total imports, and in 1823, 42 per cent were of the growth, produce, or manufacture of England and her colonies. From the British side, this meant that roughly one sixth of Britain's export was consumed by the United States. It was easy for the American merchant to avail himself of the banking and credit facilities open to British merchants and manufacturers; this fact and the basic Anglo-American exchange—raw cotton for textiles—gave the United States a somewhat colonial position in British economy. This exchange had not begun to worry American agrarians; but the manufacturers were growing restive. In 1823, however, they had not yet been able to do what Lord Liverpool so earnestly suggested that they should never do—and that was to persuade Congress to impose a protective tariff.

When the American Navigation Act of 1823, with the word "elsewhere"[2] in

[2] The word "elsewhere" referred to ports of the British Empire other than the British West

its tail, was known in England, there was more surprise than pain. It was thought that an Order-in-Council, which took immediate retaliatory measures, would speedily bring the Americans to their senses. Their Act, in short, was regarded rather as a temporary aberration than as a deliberate policy. The Order-in-Council was, of course, exceedingly firm. It provided that the shipping of the United States, when entering the ports of British colonies in North America and the West Indies, should pay a duty of 4s. 3d. per ton and of ten per cent upon their cargoes. This Order, it was thought, would soon remove the American one dollar per ton and ten per cent on the cargo, levied upon British ships: it was simply tit for tat. The Americans now seemed anxious to settle matters with a convention; and George Canning, who did not know the precise nature of Mr. Rush's instructions, probably thought at the time that this would be as good a way as any to get everyone out of their difficulties.

His behavior towards Minister Rush was, indeed, extremely affable. In July, he asked Mr. Rush to send copies of his speech of April 16 against repeal of the Foreign Enlistment Act to Mr. Monroe and Mr. Adams. These copies were corrected in Canning's own hand. In the course of the speech, he had said: "If I wished for a guide in a system of neutrality, I should take that laid down by America in the presidency of Washington and the secretaryship of Jefferson."

Now it was quite well known that Mr.

Canning did not care for Americans and that he had no love for republics. He had never, in all his private correspondence, shown any more disposition to understand or appreciate the United States than Sidney Smith had offered in his famous and bitter article in the *Edinburgh Review*.[3] In society, American gentlemen and English gentlemen did not as a rule hit it off together: and there are few examples of misunderstanding more complete than the comments privately passed upon each other by Charles Greville and Washington Irving, or by Sir Walter Scott and James Fenimore Cooper. But in the summer of 1823, Mr. Canning's formal courtesy—which he had not always been too careful to maintain—became suffused with an extraordinary warmth. The rather snobbish and rather voluble Christopher Hughes, now *chargé d'affaires* at Stockholm, happened to be passing through Liverpool on his way to St. Petersburg with dispatches; and here he met the Foreign Secretary, who had come up to his old constituency to make a speech. Canning went out of his way to shower kindnesses upon the American, and at the Mayor's banquet, where Hughes was a guest, he said of the United States and Great Britain that "the force of blood again prevails, and the daughter and the mother stand together against the world." . . .

Canning now carried his "flirtation" with the United States—as he afterwards called it—one step further. On August 16 he had a conference with Richard Rush, in the course of which Mr. Rush asked him "transiently" for his opinion on the state of affairs in Europe, adding that he derived much consolation from the thought that England would never allow France to interfere with the eman-

---

Indies. The act stated that British vessels trading to United States ports from West Indian ports shall be treated, as to duties and other charges, like United States vessels provided United States vessels were given treatment in West Indian ports similar to British vessels trading to the West Indian ports from "elsewhere."—*Ed.*

[8] *Edinburg Review*, January–March, 1820.—*Ed.*

cipation of the Spanish colonies, nor would she remain passive if France attempted to acquire territory there by conquest or cession. Canning listened gravely, and then asked what the American government would say to going hand in hand with England in such a policy. He did not think that any concert of *action* would be necessary; the simple fact of the two countries being known to hold the same opinion would, by its moral effect, check the French government in any design upon Spanish America. To this astonishing proposal the American Minister replied that he could not say in what manner his government would look upon it, but that he would communicate it in the same informal manner in which it had been thrown out. He went on to remark, very shrewdly, that much depended upon the precise situation in which the British government then stood towards the Spanish-American colonies. Were they taking, or did they think of taking any step towards the recognition of those states? This was the point, said Mr. Rush, "in which we felt the chief interest." Canning was unable to give a direct answer. He said that Great Britain was contemplating a step, not final, but preparatory, which would leave her free to "recognize or not according to the position of events at a future period." To an American, whose country was already committed to the independence of Spanish America, this would not have seemed a candid reply. Mr. Rush's very cool report of this momentous conversation was dispatched from London on August 19, and reached Washington on October 9.

On August 17, the Russian Ambassador, Count Lieven, had a long conference with Canning, in which he sought to impress upon the Foreign Secretary the foolishness of his attitude towards France. Could he not see that the French fortunes were not, after all, at a low ebb? That, on the contrary, their expedition in Spain had succeeded, and that the absolutist cause throughout Europe had received a corresponding impetus? Mr. Canning listened eagerly, and yet—it was very strange—he did not strike Lieven as being at all despondent. He replied that the time had come for him to take an active part in the new arrangements which would be made in Spain. Lieven hurried back to his wife with this news, and Madame de Lieven pondered over it, and pondered in vain. "Will his part be to arrange or to upset?" she wrote to Metternich. "We shall see." . . .

Her eager, astute, and restless mind, so brilliantly at home in the Age of Castlereagh, was still imprisoned there. She understood the politics of reaction, but the politics of the middle class entirely eluded her. She was nothing if not aristocratic. She perceived that the Liverpool-Canning-Huskisson wing of the government was firmly in the saddle, but, for the life of her, she could not realize how it had come to get there. With all her cleverness, it never occurred to her that the power now so visibly departing from Windsor Castle and the Brighton Pavilion might perhaps one day be rediscovered in the Manchester Chamber of Commerce.

Mr. Canning, therefore, was well established at home. . . . At the same time, his diplomacy, there was no denying it, had suffered an obvious setback. In September, the French army was approaching Cadiz where Ferdinand VII, the prisoner of the Constitutionalists, lay idly meditating revenge and tribulation. On August 20 Mr. Canning wrote a note to Mr. Rush, in which he stated in "unofficial and confidential" terms that

1. We conceive the recovery of the Colonies by Spain to be hopeless.
2. We conceive the question of the Recognition of them, as Independent States, to be one of time and circumstance.
3. We are, however, by no means disposed to throw any impediment in the way of an arrangement between them and the mother country by amicable negotiations.
4. We aim not at the possession of any portion of them ourselves.
5. We could not see any portion of them transferred to any other Power with indifference.

"If these opinions and feelings are [he added], as I firmly believe them to be, common to your government with ours, why should we hesitate mutually to confide them with each other; and to declare them in the face of the world? . . . Do you conceive that under the power which you have recently received, you are authorized to enter into negotiation, and to sign any Convention upon this subject? . . . Nothing would be more gratifying to me than to join with you in such a work, and, I am persuaded, there has seldom, in the history of the world, occurred an opportunity, when so small an effort, of two friendly Governments, might produce so unequivocal a good and prevent such extensive calamities." The flirtation had become a courtship.

Mr. Rush replied, three days later, that his government fully agreed with the sentiments in Mr. Canning's note, but that the paramount consideration must be the reception of the Spanish-American states into the family of nations by the powers of Europe, "and especially, I may add, by Great Britain." His instructions, he said, did not permit him to commit his government in advance; and he con-

tented himself with remarking that it would give him particular pleasure to bring Mr. Canning's views before the President as promptly as he could. Mr. Canning, however, had just received word that, as soon as the French campaign was over, a new European Congress would be called to deal especially with the affairs of Spanish America. "I need not point out," he said in a letter from Liverpool, which crossed Mr. Rush's in the mail, "all the complications to which this proposal, however dealt with by us, may lead." All he received by way of answer was the familiar hint that if the British government would fully acknowledge the independence of the Spanish-American states, "it would accelerate the steps of my government (and) it would also naturally place *me* in a new position in my further conferences with you, on this interesting subject."

If Rush had succeeded in forcing the British to recognize the Spanish Americans, he was then honestly prepared to go through with his part of the bargain —that is to say, "to make a declaration in the name of my government that it will not remain inactive under an attack upon the independence of those states by the Holy Alliance," and to make this declaration explicitly and avow it before the world. He was well aware that, in thus exceeding his instructions, he might be disavowed by his own government; but he was prepared to take all the blame upon himself, and to sweeten his disgrace with the thought that he had acted for the best. In these very anxious days, with no one to advise him, his actions were astonishingly cool and brave. Canning answered from Westmoreland that he could not bind himself and his colleagues —whose sentiments he had been expressing as well as his own—simply on the

American Minister's word without the support of positive instructions from Washington: in other words, that the British government was not yet ready for an immediate recognition. Mr. Rush at first seemed to think that this unwillingness to negotiate on the basis of equivalents—recognition for co-operation— would bring the whole business to an end. But as day followed day without another word from Canning, who was due to return to London in the middle of September, he changed his mind; he thought that the Foreign Secretary would renew his conversations with all his former urgency; and, while preparing his mind for this encounter, he wrote a very strange letter to President Monroe.

He told the President that he deeply mistrusted the Tory government. It was true that they had lately become very liberal in their foreign-trade policy, and he believed that they would become more so. But he did not think that they had changed in their attitude towards political freedom, or that a change, if it took place, would be of a sort to invite the confidence and co-operation of the United States. Great Britain had fought the Napoleonic Wars, ostensibly in support of the freedom of other states, but actually against the people of France. She had aided the Holy Alliance, either positively or negatively, until the Alliance seemed to threaten her commercial interests in Spanish America and her political sway in both hemispheres. She would continue to act the part "which she acted in 1774 in America, which she has since acted in Europe, and is now acting in Ireland. . . . I shall therefore find it hard," he wrote, "to keep from my mind the suspicion that the approaches of her ministers to me at this portentous juncture for a concert of policy which they

have not heretofore courted with the United States, are bottomed on their own calculations."

Mr. Rush knew as well as anyone that diplomatic approaches are rarely if ever "bottomed" on anything else. He hastened to add that he did not accuse the British Cabinet, "as it is now composed," of any sinister motives toward the United States. On the contrary, he believed that Lord Liverpool and Mr. Canning would advocate an even more intimate and friendly policy towards them, "no matter from what motives arising." He did not think that the Whigs or the Radicals would ever offer such good terms.

This letter, with its odd alternations of suspicion and speculation, is an admirable example of the effect of the new Liberal Toryism upon a shrewd observer. Mr. Rush was not, like Madame de Lieven, simply bewildered. He saw very clearly that a government might have no respect for civil liberties but still might show a high regard for commercial advantages. He perceived rather less clearly that a British foreign policy based on the conservation of wealth was gradually being superseded by a British foreign policy dedicated to the enlargement of opportunity. He did not believe that the friendly overtures of Mr. Canning were due entirely to a British anxiety for South American markets. He was not sure what other motives might lie behind these overtures, and he was evidently surprised that a Tory Cabinet should be making them—so surprised, indeed, that he could only suppose that a Whig or a Radical Cabinet would be "the decided opponents of such a policy." He did not realize that British statesmen were not their own masters; that all would follow, willingly or unwillingly, wherever the Industrial Revolution led them. In 1823, the Industrial Revolution was not a recognizable concept.

Mr. Rush never lost his head, but he grew more puzzled and suspicious. It is well to remember that he was to become a Protectionist Secretary of the Treasury under John Quincy Adams, and that it was a Tory Prime Minister, Sir Robert Peel, who, years later, dealt the final blow for British Free Trade. There was a prophecy in Rush's letter to Monroe but, like most prophecies, it was indistinct.

At any rate, when George Canning reappeared in London he did fulfill one of Richard Rush's predictions. He renewed his overtures and he imparted to them a degree of warmth which still surprises us, coming as they did from a man who disliked republics only a little less than he despised republicans. He said that the United States were the first power established on the American continent, "and now confessedly the leading Power. Had not a new epoch arrived in the relative position of the United States toward Europe, which Europe must acknowledge? Were the great political and commercial interests which hung upon the destinies of the new continent, to be canvassed and adjusted in this hemisphere, without the co-operation or even knowledge of the United States? Where they to be canvassed and adjusted, he would even add, without some proper understanding between the United States and Great Britain, *as the two chief commercial and maritime states of both worlds?* He hoped not, he would wish to persuade himself not." These were seductive words; but the cautious Rush still hung back. He replied that if he were to task the risk of entangling the United States in the affairs of

Europe, he must have some justification beyond any that had yet been laid before him. At this, Mr. Canning grew lyrical. "Why . . . should the United States, whose institutions always, and whose policy in this instance, approximated them so much more closely to Great Britain than to any other power in Europe, hesitate to act with her to promote a common object approved alike by both?" No British statesman, while in office, had hitherto been able to detect a close resemblance between the institutions of the United States and those of Great Britain. It only remained for Mr. Canning to declare that if he were invited to the European Congress, he would decline to appear unless the United States were invited also. He could go no further. But he received the same stubborn answer: if he would pledge his government to an immediate recognition of the South American states, Mr. Rush would sign a joint declaration on Spanish America. But the economic wing of the British government, strong as it was, was not yet strong enough to force the whole Cabinet into such an open break with the Powers of Europe; nor would it do so, in any case, as long as the Spanish Constitutionalists were in the field. Eight days after this remarkable interview, which took place on September 18, Canning made a last effort: he summoned Rush to Gloucester Lodge and asked him if "a promise by England of *future* acknowledgment" would satisfy his scruples; but the answer was the same as before. When they met again on October 8 and October 9, not a word was said about co-operation with regard to Spanish America: nor did they ever speak of it again.

The great courtship was ended, and for a very simple reason: there was no longer any time for dalliance. On September 30

Cadiz fell to the French, and the Revolution was over. This news did not reach London until October 10, but Canning had already taken steps to soften its consequences. He believed that the French contemplated a direct interference in Spanish America, certainly with ships and perhaps with soldiers. He did not think for a moment that they could succeed in this venture against the opposition of British sea power. But, as Foreign Secretary, he could not watch with complacency or without fear this resounding victory for the reactionaries of Europe. On October 3, he began a series of conversations with Prince Jules de Polignac, the French Ambassador, which resulted in the great Polignac Memorandum of October 9 to 12, 1823. In this Memorandum, the British government declared that they regarded the reduction of Spanish America to its ancient submission as hopeless; that they would not interfere in any practicable negotiation between Spain and the colonies; but that "the junction of any Foreign Power in an enterprise of Spain against the Colonies, would be viewed by them as constituting an entirely new question, and one upon which they must take such decision as the interests of Great Britain would require." To this exceedingly strong language there were added certain trade requirements of vital significance. The British government maintained that ever since 1810 the trade with the Spanish colonies had been open to British subjects, and that the ancient coast laws of Spain were "as regarded them at least, racially repealed." Great Britain did not ask for a separate right to this trade: the force of circumstances and the "irreversible progress of events" had already made it free to all the world; but if her claim were disputed she would immediately recognize the independence of the Spanish-American states. The Prince de Polignac replied that France, on her part, disclaimed any intention or desire to appropriate to herself any part of the Spanish possessions in America; that she asked for nothing more than the right to trade in Spanish America upon the same terms as Great Britain ("to rank, after the Mother Country, among the most favored nations"); and that she "adjured, in any case, any design of acting against the colonies by force of arms."

It is evident that here was at least as much of an agreement on trade rights as of a warning to France against aggression. None the less, its language was decisive. . . .

The drama of the Rush-Canning conversations—for they *were* dramatic—lies in the interplay of the conscious and the unconscious motives in Canningite diplomacy. Consciously, no doubt, Canning wished above all to extract from the United States, in the course of the joint declaration, a pledge never to seize the island of Cuba. Then again, he thought that he could offset his diplomatic defeats in Europe by coming to a public understanding with America. He also feared that the French might revive their colonial empire and their old sea power; and he perceived in the purchasers of Louisiana the most eloquent opponents, with England, of such an ambition. He was concerned about the freedom of the South American trade and he knew that the United States, more than any other nation except France, shared this anxiety. And he was eager to "prevent the drawing of the line of demarcation which I most dread—America versus Europe."

All these were powerful reasons for an overture to the United States; all were unquestionably present in his mind; yet all together do not quite satisfy the conditions necessary for so urgent a plea to

Rush. He had learned from Stratford Canning that the United States did not intend to seize Cuba, either then or in the near future. He could hardly have persuaded himself that the United States meant a great deal to the Powers of Europe. He was quite convinced that British sea power could sink any expedition, whether French or Holy, long before it reached Spanish America. As for the future of the South American market, how much better to stand forth as the single defender of Spanish America, not by an act of recognition, but by simply threatening the aggressors with the British navy! Nor could he have concealed from himself that a line of demarcation would be more easily drawn by tariffs than expunged by joint declarations. Every reason had a counter reason; but Mr. Canning pressed on.

The very essence of Lord Liverpool's government can be discovered in its instinctive response to the demands of industry; and this was strange, since Lord Liverpool's party was a party of landed proprietors, to whom the demands of industry meant less than nothing. The manner of this response was one of arid paternalism: Lord Liverpool's government led the way, it did not conceive itself as yielding to pressure. Its reforms were practical, common-sense reforms; and if they were tentative, that was because it was a pioneer and an experimenter, working against immense obstacles and in an economy not fully developed. Lord Liverpool had always to calm the Ultra Tory members of his own Cabinet. William Huskisson's assault upon the silk monopoly was conducted in despite of the best manufacturing opinion. And even Huskisson proposed no more than a modification of the Navigation Laws and the tariff schedules; even

his free trade opinions, vigorous and transforming though they were, were only the leaven in a lump of mild protectionism. In one respect, moreover, all the leading reformers in this singular government—Liverpool, Canning, Huskisson, Robinson—were very Tory indeed: all were opponents of Parliamentary reform.

None the less, the instinct of an industrial economy, hovering upon the edge of an unparalleled expansion, is always to make friends with friendly, free, and subservient markets; and this instinct seized upon Lord Liverpool and his liberal colleagues, using them for its own mysterious ends. When the merchants of London, the Chamber of Commerce of Glasgow, the woolen manufacturers of Howick, and the manufacturers of Manchester and Birmingham appealed to Parliament in 1820 for a greater freedom of trade, Lord Liverpool replied with his blunt suggestion that the prosperity of England depended upon the prosperity of a tariff-free United States. He did not direct the foreign policy of George Canning; but he supported and encouraged it, in Parliament and out. And George Canning approached Richard Rush not only as the conscious diplomatist but also as the partly unconscious servant of the energies of British coal and iron, of British spindles and furnaces. Nor was his plea simply directed towards the safety of Cuba or the enlargement of South American trade: it was also, and more so, a wooing of the free North American market—a diplomatic extension, in a moment of crisis, of Lord Liverpool's 1820 speech. It was aimed, in brief, ultimately and instinctively at the agrarian mind of the United States; or at that portion of the agrarian mind which was contented with the exchange of staples for manufactures.

Did Monroe's unilateral declaration close the door to cooperation with Great Britain? Both Perkins and Whitaker suggest in their studies that the idea of association with Britain was not entirely repudiated. It remained, however, for GALE W. McGEE (1915–   ) to elaborate on the theme and document it from the writings of Rush, Monroe, Adams, Jefferson, and Canning. McGee, trained at Chicago, taught United States diplomatic history at the University of Wyoming until 1958, when he was elected United States senator from Wyoming. His article served as an important corrective to the popularly held view that Monroe and Adams rejected Canning's overtures categorically. He contends that the declaration was a stopgap measure pending an arrangement with London.*

An Arrangement with London to Follow Monroe's Declaration

The Monroe Doctrine has generally been looked upon as a unilateral policy, deliberately accepted by the United States in preference to an "entangling" British suggestion of a joint manifesto. The doctrine of the two spheres, moreover, has commonly been associated with the principles of isolationism. But both the determination of the Americans to "go it alone" and the attributes of isolation become apparent only when certain utterances of the principal statesmen involved are lifted from the context of the diplomatic conditions which produced them.

If those statements are left in their context it is possible to see that while the early spokesmen often voiced a desire to remain unfettered, they seldom permitted their ideals to blind them to realities. With a sagacity rarely equaled since then, they stood ever ready to compromise ideals with the exigencies of reality in order to obtain what was to them more fundamental than any theories of nonentanglement—the security of the nation. In the discussions which evoked the Monroe Doctrine this is clearly illustrated.

Long before George Canning became alarmed over the designs of the Holy Alliance in the New World, the Ameri-

---

* Gale W. McGee, "The Monroe Doctrine—A Stopgap Measure," *Mississippi Valley Historical Review*, 38 (1951), 233–250. Reprinted without footnotes by permission of the author and the Mississippi Valley Historical Association.

cans were concerning themselves with the threat. After turning down the repeated invitations of the Czar to accede to his European concert, the United States served notice that it would have nothing to do with any scheme for restoring Spanish control in South America. As early as December, 1815, Secretary of State James Monroe instructed John Quincy Adams, then minister to Britain, to sound the London government on the question of recognizing the independence of the Latin-American nations. Although nothing came of the gesture, Monroe as president made it the business of a cabinet session three years later, in May, 1818. From his official family he sought advice as to whether measures ought to be taken to ascertain Britain's attitude toward a concert of policies in which any project affecting the Latin Americans should receive no support unless the end result would be independence. The upshot of the cabinet session was an instruction to Richard Rush, minister to London, which Secretary of State Adams drafted:

It may be an interesting object of your attention to watch the moment when this idea [cooperation with Britain in recognizing the independence of Latin America] will become prevalent in the British councils, and to encourage any disposition which may consequently be manifested to a more perfect concert of measures between the United States and Great Britain towards that end— the total independence of the Spanish South American provinces.

Nor was this informal proposal permitted to lapse. Two months later Monroe "very abruptly" asked Adams to propose to the British minister, Charles Bagot, joint action to aid the ambitions of the Spanish colonies for independence. Although the Secretary thought the English were not yet ready to assume such an advanced position in American affairs, the proposal was not abandoned. It was translated into a formal proposition and transmitted to the Court of London in August, 1818. As it read, the proposal was "for a concerted and contemporary recognition of the independence of Buenos Ayres." In refusing the offer, the British said only that it did not then suit their policy.

The Americans, however, were not to be easily discouraged. In the following December joint action in recognizing Buenos Aires was suggested both to London and Paris. Although neither overture evoked favorable sentiment, they were followed closely by the most definite offer to originate in Washington. In January, 1819, President Monroe, encouraged by the British refusal at the Congress of Aix-la-Chapelle to intervene in the Spanish colonies, brought the issue before his cabinet once again. On January 2, when Adams showed Monroe a dispatch prepared for Rush announcing the intention of the government to recognize the independence of Brazil, the President declared his opposition to a unilateral act, preferring to follow rather than oppose the current of European politics. In the cabinet, where Adams objected to any "deference to England," Secretary of War John C. Calhoun voiced the prevailing sentiment in expressing "the most earnestness to avoid acting unless in concert with England." As a consequence, the Secretary of State's original dispatch was altered to say that in Washington it was hoped that the difference between the views of the two English-speaking nations was one of form rather than substance. The new instructions said in part, "If it should suit the views of Great Britain to adopt similar measures at the same time and in concert with us, it will be highly satisfactory to the President." The offer, however, was accorded a cold reception by Lord Castlereagh.

Further manifestations of a disposition in the United States to combine policies with the British appeared in 1821. Stratford Canning, His Majesty's minister in Washington, reported this to Castlereagh as the substance of an April conference with Adams. On that occasion the Secretary of State said that he personally "should view with pleasure anything which tended even to draw closer the amicable relations of the two countries." The mere tone of these opening remarks caught the British by surprise, since it was somewhat of a reversal of form on the part of Adams.

"I inquired of Mr. Adams," reported Canning, "whether . . . the terms which he had just used were directed to any particular object." He was told that nothing specific was contemplated. There was a new series of events just commencing in Europe, Adams explained, and "circumstances, affording ground for a closer connection might possibly arise in the course of their development." Coupled with the shift on the European political front was the added fact of new uprisings in Latin America. As a result of these conversations, Stratford Canning concluded that Adams was intimating "a readiness to *receive* any proposal from Great Britain."

At approximately the same time, and coincident with Adams' startling gesture to the British minister, Richard Rush reported from London that English policy toward the Holy Alliance was preceptibly more frigid. Mutual interest, it would appear, was driving the two English-speaking governments onto common ground.

By early 1823 the events of European politics were nudging the Anglo-Americans even closer together. The suddenness with which France in that year forcibly deposed the liberal government in Spain alarmed officials both in Washington and London. Even the suspicious Adams sensed the growing friendship. As Stratford Canning reported it to his cousin in the foreign office, George Canning, the apparent determination of Great Britain to oppose the South American ambitions of the Holy Alliance had made "the English almost popular in the United States," with Adams himself having "caught a something of the soft infection."

The American Secretary of State in effect seemed to have executed a neat about-face in his attitude toward the British. Commenting on the "coincidence of principle" existing between the two governments, he went so far as to suggest to Stratford Canning that the two might compare their "ideas and purposes together, with a view to the accommodation of great interests upon which they had hitherto differed." This was further indicated in the tone of the instructions prepared for Richard Rush in July, 1823. As Adams explained the substance of the new orders to His Majesty's minister in Washington, they had been drawn "with a view . . . of establishing a common understanding, on several points affecting the interests of the two Countries." Rush was informed that in regard to the proposed negotiation, "the final result anxiously looked to from it . . . [was] a more permanent and harmonious concert of public policy and community of purpose between our two countries, than has ever yet existed since the period of our independence."

It is apparent that by midsummer of 1823 Great Britain and the United States were close to a concert of policies. Both the time and the European setting were propitious for George Canning's overtures to Richard Rush; his "spectacular" proposals did not come out of a clear sky. They had a sound basis in the early efforts of the United States to team up with Britain on Latin America. They had an immediate source in the unusual American cordiality toward England manifesting itself in the spring and summer months of 1823. And finally, they were a logical consequence of the coincidental secession of Great Britain from the concert of Europe and the mounting American suspicion of the Holy Alliance.

The substance of Canning's conversations with Richard Rush during August and September of 1823 are too well known to need repeating. Let it be borne in mind, however, that by late September the distance separating the two men from some sort of joint commitment was surprisingly small. It could be measured by the distance between Canning's suggestion that Rush accept a British pledge for the *future* recognition of South American independence and Rush's insistence upon a British policy of *immediate* recognition.

The crest of the tide of an Anglo-American diplomatic understanding was actually reached in the conference of September 26, destined to be the last exchange on the subject in London for nearly two months. The British foreign minister, in the meantime, would elicit from the French government, through Count Polignac, convincing assurances

that France would not participate in an overseas expedition in behalf of the Spanish colonial interests. As a result Canning beat a hasty retreat from the position he had assumed in his talks with the American envoy.

In Washington, however, the tempo of official opinion on the question of an Anglo-American accommodation was on the increase, and continued so during October and November. The government there was not to learn until February of the following year that in London the project had been abandoned.

When the British proposition was received by James Monroe, it touched off a series of spirited discussions among the President and his advisers. In the eyes of Thomas Jefferson it was the most "momentous" development since 1776, and to John Quincy Adams it seemed to be "Of such magnitude, such paramount consequence, as involving the whole future policy of the United States."

As a consequence of the official deliberations the American government manifested a disposition toward a policy of action which deviated substantially from the tenets usually associated with the Monroe Doctrine. That disposition constitutes a significant chapter in the origins of United States foreign policy. In order to keep in mind the contemporary setting from which the Monroe message evolved, it is well to recall the better known comments on the proposed policy of collaboration with Great Britain. President Monroe first of all sought the advice of two of the country's elder statesmen, his fellow Virginians and predecessors in office, Jefferson and Madison.

Thomas Jefferson stressed that while our true objective should be to make the western hemisphere the "domicile . . . of freedom," separate from Europe, yet, in attaining that objective, "One nation, most of all, could disturb us . . . , she now offers to lead, aid, and accompany us in it." By acceding to the proposal, moreover, Britain would be detached from the European system. Even should a war result from the rapprochement, he added, such a war would not be "her war, but ours." To James Madison, joining with the British would be a wise step "short of war." But for him this was not enough. He would have the two English-speaking peoples issue a similar declaration in behalf of the Greeks.

Nor was James Monroe hesitant about what should be done. While no foreign entanglements was a sound policy, he said, the present seemed to justify a departure from it. "My own impression is," he observed, "that we ought to meet the proposal of the British govt. & to make it known, that we would view an interference on the part of the European powers . . . as an attack on ourselves, presuming that, if they succeeded with them, they would extend it to us."

With the exception of John Quincy Adams, the cabinet members were pretty much agreed upon the threat and only slightly less so upon a course of action. The President favored giving Rush discretionary powers to effect a merging of policy with the British. Secretary of War Calhoun believed sufficient powers should be sent to permit an accession to all of Canning's proposals, and if necessary, even to the point of relinquishing ambitions in Cuba and Texas. . . .

But around none of the cabinet members has tradition spun a more romantic narrative than about the Secretary of State. Never one to hunt with the pack, it was natural that John Quincy Adams would hold divergent views. The conventional accounts of his courageous efforts to steer the administration along a course of true Americanism and independent action are well known. From his own accounts we learn that he alone opposed joining with Britain. His reasons are significant. Strongly suspicious of Canning's motives, he felt that some ulterior objects were being entertained. These he thought to include an intention of blocking the further expansionist efforts of the United States to the southward.

He regarded the threat from the Holy Alliance, moreover, as more fancied than real. Though willing to concede that the Allies "might make a temporary impression [in Latin America] for three, four, or five years," he thought it no more probable that the Spanish dominions could be restored to the mother country "than that the Chimborazo will sink beneath the ocean." Believing that self-interest rather than adherence to idealistic principles would finally regulate the conduct of the courts of Europe, he could discern no practical basis upon which they could rest a policy of intervention in behalf of Spain.

While inclined to minimize the threat from abroad, Adams, nevertheless, was ready to act on the question proposed by Canning. What concerned him most was that England was already disposed to act, in which case it would appear to the outside world that she had taken the lead; to her, thus, would fall the credit for preserving the interests of the western hemisphere. To England, as a result, would accrue commercial favors, probably at the expense of the United States. For this reason the Secretary of State observed that "It would be more candid, as well as more dignified, to avow our principles explicitly to Russia and France, than to come in as a cock-boat in the wake of a British man-of-war."

Nowhere among his utterances at this point does Adams reveal a determination to reject the Canning overture on account of tradition or its entangling consequences. From his own phrases, in fact, one can arrive at the not unwarranted conclusion that collaboration was acceptable to him provided it neither barred America's future ambitions in Cuba nor relegated the United States to the position of an appendage to British policy.

Other indications that Adams was not as staunchly set against collaborating with the British as convention would have it are revealed in the dispatches of His Majesty's charge in Washington Henry U. Addington. While Canning had been sounding Rush in London, Addington was pushing essentially the same proposition in conversations with Adams. These efforts had begun perhaps in late September when Canning perceived that he was getting nowhere with Rush. At any rate, by the first of November Addington and Adams held a conference at which the subject was a "joint manifesto on Spanish America." And shortly thereafter, at a dinner party, the British envoy received an account of the Rush-Canning exchanges from the American Secretary of State. With the proposition, reported Addington, "Mr. Adams seemed extremely gratified, and evidently contemplated his country as already placed by it on a much higher elevation than that on which she had hitherto stood."

The following weeks brought no satisfactory agreement between the two. The diplomatic exchanges, however, fail to disclose any mounting hostility on the part of Adams. They reveal, on the contrary, a disposition on his part to accede to the proposal from London. This is apparent in the detailed account of the several conversations which Addington forwarded to his chief in Britain during December. On an occasion subsequent to the dinner party already alluded to, Adams again adverted to the Canning offer. "Mr. Adams was also evidently much pleased with the manner in which the proposition had been made, as well as the opening thus afforded for his Country to play so prominent a part in the affairs of the World," Addington recorded. But when pressed for an immediate decision so that the compact might operate as a "preventive," the Secretary asked for more time, pleading the "paramount consequence" of the rapprochement.

Calling again in a few days, Addington was once more put off. Adams advised him, however, that the terms laid down by Rush in London were those which the administration would insist upon. The critical issue, of course, was the matter of recognition. Without that acknowledgment "no durable concert and harmony of operations could be looked for," Adams declared, but "let one common basis be laid down, and there would be no longer any difficulty in concerting common measures." The Secretary of State extended a concession, moreover, as if to facilitate the conclusion of the pact. If Great Britain would only recognize one country, he told Addington, so as to lay down the principle, he would accede to Canning's proposition.

Once again, on November 19, the British diplomat inquired whether the necessary instructions would be sent to Rush in the November 24 packet. Adams, who had received him "with unusual affability," replied that, "for himself, he was quite ready, but the President might possibly desire more time to reflect on a matter of such deep importance." He hastened to add, then, that "the United States were warmly and cordially disposed to make common cause with Great Britain," provided only that recognition came first.

Finally, Addington made one last effort, this on December 1, only to discover that the decision was still pending. The subject, Adams explained, "was a more complicated one" than at first believed. But even without British recognition, he assured the visiting diplomat that "The United States would show by acts how cordially they concurred in the line of policy proposed to be pursued by Great Britain." On taking his leave the Britisher noted that the American Secretary "concluded by expressing in terms of warmth and apparent sincerity, his earnest hope that the relations which existed between our two governments would become daily of a closer and more confidential nature."

It would appear that most students of the Monroe Doctrine have overlooked or ignored this Addington dispatch. That document suggests that the conventional accounts which have ascribed to Adams the airs of a knight-errant bent upon preserving independence of action for America perhaps should be modified. The Secretary of State possibly was not as much opposed to the British overture as is usually thought. How much of what he told Addington was personal conviction and how much was sheer diplomatic palaver cannot be precisely determined, of course. But Adams was not one to equivocate; if anything, his bluntness had on occasion plagued him.

It can be seen, therefore, that among government advisers there was a strong inclination in favor of a joint pronouncement with Great Britain. Disagreement existed principally on the specific conditions governing such a declaration. In the light of this disposition it becomes exceedingly difficult to account for Monroe's message of December 2 as one reflecting an American determination to "go it alone." Some other explanation is called for.

Although the American government had learned from Richard Rush that Canning had cooled toward his own proposal, at no time before the Monroe message to Congress, did it regard the negotiations as having been broken off. There is interesting evidence, on the contrary, which indicates that the President's famous pronouncement was issued as a provisional measure—a stopgap, designed not only to secure for the United States a proper share of the responsibility and credit for looking after hemispheric interests, but also to fill the immediate requirements of world diplomacy —namely, holding the line against the Holy Alliance until the Canning-Rush conversations could be translated into a binding agreement.

It was not until November 29 that the new set of instructions which Rush had requested for guidance in dealing with Canning's overtures were ready to be sent to the American minister in London. Endorsing the envoy's own replies to the British diplomat, the directive stipulated that Britain must first recognize the independence of the new governments of South America. With the Anglo-Americans then occupying like ground, the United States would be willing "to move in concert with Great Britain for the purposes specified."

For the time being, however, Rush was advised that the two nations should act separately, effecting a common policy through close consultations. But, "should an emergency occur, in which a *joint* manifestation of opinion . . . may tend to influence the Councils of the European Allies," he was to notify his own government immediately. In that event, the instructions concluded, "We shall according to the principles of our Government, and in the forms prescribed by our Constitution, cheerfully join in any act by which we may contribute to support the cause of human freedom, and the Independence of the South American Nations."

The instructions bear upon American policy in two respects. First, they show that the Monroe government was wary of a sweeping commitment from which the British might retreat or fail to carry through. If Britain could be forced to recognize the Latin Americans the likelihood of their deserting the Yankees would be lessened since it would cost Britain her usual ally in Europe, Spain, and leave her to depend upon the Americans. That is why the statesmen in Washington demanded immediate recognition. In the face of the sudden coolness on the part of Canning as disclosed by Rush's dispatch of October 10, this action does not seem to have been unreasonable.

But perhaps an even more significant revelation in the instructions is the apparent belief that the negotiations on the question of joint action would continue. That the United States either expected, or hoped for, the resumption of the talks is clearly manifested in the endorsement of Rush's demand for prior recognition. This is illustrated further by the suggestion advanced in the orders which looked to the transfer of subsequent negotiations to Washington, where the projected entente was even then a topic of conversation between Adams and Addington. The United States, it would appear, was carefully keeping the door open for a future arrangement.

It is, of course, impossible to say with certainty that the Monroe government was doing any more than probe for possible ulterior motives in British policy. But several hints and private opinions contained in the correspondence of individuals close to the administration indicate that the intent was something more than exploratory. From no quarter was this more apparent than in the White House itself.

Even after his message to Congress had been delivered, the President continued to worry over Canning's sudden coolness. On December 4 he wrote to Jefferson that in the face of the mounting threat from the Holy Alliance, "the most unpleasant circumstance . . . is that Mr. Canning's zeal has much abated of late." Just why, he was not sure, but he ascribed it either to the question of recognition being pressed so strongly by Rush, or to counteroffers made by the Allies to "seduce" the British. Monroe, it should be noted, while regarding Canning's interest as having "abated," did not look upon it as having died. He suggested at least a hope that the negotiations with London might be continued.

This is borne out further by the tone of another set of instructions sent to Rush on December 8. Aroused by the rumor that Cadiz had fallen to France, a development which would release an Allied army of 12,500 to assault Spanish America, the President, Rush was told, was "anxiously desirous that the opening to a cordial harmony in the policy of the United States and Great Britain, offered on this occasion . . . [might be] extended to the general Relations between the two countries." The time required for the Allies to prepare the anticipated expedition, the orders concluded, "may yet be employed, if necessary, by Great Britain and the United States, in a further concert of operations, to counter-act that design, if really entertained."

In a still later letter to Jefferson the President disclosed his belief that a rapprochement was still in the offing. After alluding to the continuing threat of the European concert, he reverted to an Anglo-American entente as the best means to guard against it. But to effect such a collaboration, he observed, it had best emanate from the United States in order to avoid the appearance that his government was only the instrument of England.

Another letter to Jefferson, written nearly six weeks after the statement to Congress—January 12, 1824—discloses that Monroe was even at that late date still waiting for more news on Canning's proposal. "Since my last," wrote the President, "we have receiv'd no communication from Mr. Rush, on the subject of Mr. Cannings proposition." Quite obviously he did not view the British project as having been dropped. . . .

As late as December 26, 1823, Madison was still counseling a joint policy with the British, and this to President Monroe. The principal limitation, he suggested, would be to prevent the London government from usurping "a meritorious lead" in any action in behalf of our South American neighbors. "Nor ought we to be less careful in guarding against an appearance in the eyes of Europe, at which the self-love of Great Britain

may aim, of our being a satellite of her primary interests." Given these precautionary policies, however, then cooperation should not only be accepted, it should be sought. This particular letter is not only important for what it reveals of Madison's views on the Monroe declaration, but even more important in that it was written to the President of the United States, suggesting that the latter was thinking along the same lines.

In the records of the House of Representatives, also, there is additional evidence. Nearly two months after the famous Declaration was issued, Congressman Alexander Smyth of Virginia, in House debate on the Greek question, sought to clarify what the President had intended on December 2. Those remarks precluded our extending material aid to Greece, because it would be "going out of our way to beard the Allies: to seek a quarrel with them respecting the affairs of Europe," he explained, the effect of which would be to "make the declaration of the President . . . a falsehood." To remain within the bounds of the December 2 statements, we should let England carry the torch in Europe. But we should not stand idly by if Britian is attacked by the Allies; "if she is involved in a war with the Allies, for the independence of nations, we ought to give her assurance that we will not be neutral, but will give her faithful and honorable support." According to Smyth, then, while the Monroe message barred our taking the lead in settling the quarrels of Europe, it had not closed the door to an Anglo-American understanding.

By February, 1824, however, the Americans learned that there would be no rapprochement with their English cousins. Rush's November dispatch telling of Canning's explanations for dropping the project reached Washington on February 2. No longer was it necessary to speculate on the form of a policy of joint action.

The whole series of diplomatic exchanges surrounding the Monroe Doctrine have an important bearing on the formulation of American foreign policy. While they reveal a laudable determination to avert becoming a mere tail to the British diplomatic kite, they also disclose a strong disposition toward a collaboration with the English. James Monroe's message of December 2, 1823, it would also appear, was not intended as a refusal of Canning's bid. Nor can it be said with complete accuracy that the pronouncement was made in the knowledge that the original offer had been abandoned. The American government had continued to act with the expectation that discussions on the project would be continued, an assumption which prevailed until February 2, 1824.

In the light of the foregoing materials, the following conclusions in regard to those statements in President James Monroe's message to Congress December 2, 1823, subsequently to be called the Monroe Doctrine, would seem to be in order. (1) The idea for a policy of joint action in Latin America evolved as much from American initiative before 1823 as from George Canning's overtures to Richard Rush in August of that year.

(2) The Canning project was viewed with less hostility by the policy makers in the United States, including John Quincy Adams, than has been generally recognized. (3) The message itself appears to have been a temporary expedient—a stopgap measure intended to hold the line against the designs of Europe while the diplomatic conversations begun by Canning and Rush in London could be continued. (4) In part, it may have been a move to insure to the United States at least an equal share of the credit which might follow a joint manifesto in behalf of the former Spanish colonies in the New World. (5) It was issued with the expectation that there would be further negotiations on the British proposal for some sort of collaboration, and was not intended as a negative reply to the offer from England.

Viewed in this light, the objectives of the Monroe Doctrine seem to be very different from those alleged by students who have tried to see in its enunciation the spirit of "isolation." Quite on the contrary, it would appear that the statesmen in Washington felt that isolation, in fact, was impossible. Instead of pledging themselves to a "tradition," they dedicated their efforts to the most fundamental question of all—that of American security. To achieve that end they were prepared for close cooperation with Great Britain.

Bolivian born (1900–   ) and American educated, RAÚL DIEZ DE MEDINA is both diplomat and writer. He has served his country in many posts abroad and has written a number of books on hemisphere affairs. *Autopsy of the Monroe Doctrine,* from which the following selection is drawn, was his master of science thesis, written in 1934 and published under the pseudonym GASTON NERVAL. The book is an indictment of the Doctrine as an egoistic and unilateral policy. The selection, entitled "Castles in the Air," serves to demonstrate that from the beginning the Doctrine was not useful to Latin Americans. It describes the dashed hopes and disappointments of South Americans in the years immediately following the message when Washington rebuffed their requests for assistance.*

Egoistic from Its Pronouncement

The real, the original Monroe Doctrine is not so difficult to define. We have today a more or less complete knowledge of the circumstances which brought it about, and of the manner and spirit in which it was first advanced. We also have the statements and interpretations of public men of the time, who were in direct contact with the conditions that called forth the Doctrine and whose testimony, therefore, is the only one we can accept as that of "material witnesses." . . . The chief motive behind the message of December 2, 1823, was the security of the United States. In the words of Professor Hart, the Doctrine could be understood only *"as a statement of a right of self-protection against action by foreign powers.* The main purpose of the Doctrine was to prevent disturbances to our institutions and to minimize dangers to the United States."

What we must establish, now, is whether this view prevailed with the statesmen of the United States after the issuance of the Monroe Doctrine— whether the safety and the political interests of the United States continued to be the deciding factor in the interpretation of the Doctrine. The answer to this question will give us a clue to understand what the original Monroe Doctrine really is—or, rather, what it was intended to

---

* From Gaston Nerval, *Autopsy of the Monroe Doctrine,* pp. 116–126. New York: The Macmillan Company, 1934. Reprinted without footnotes by permission of the author.

be—and, more important still, what it is not.

Nothing will serve better our purpose, in this connection, than a brief account of the early attempts made by various Latin American governments to give the Monroe Doctrine a contractual character, widening its scope, and of the stern, unyielding refusal of the United States which killed those attempts.

The message of President Monroe was welcomed with great rejoicing throughout Latin America. Not knowing the inside story of the diplomatic negotiations which preceded it, not knowing the weakness of the European menace at that time, not knowing the real purpose of the Washington government in advancing it, the people of Latin America attributed to the Monroe Doctrine a degree of altruism and effectiveness far above reality. Only through the glass of this popular delusion, the efforts of the most important Latin American governments of the epoch to participate in the privileges and obligations of the Doctrine may be understood. They evidently over-estimated the generosity of their Northern neighbor and misunderstood its aims. But they could not be blamed for it. Those were not the days of diplomacy behind open doors.

Their mistaken optimism, on the other hand, and the disappointment which it caused them, served to clarify the real nature of the Monroe declarations and to establish even then, at the very beginning, the light in which the United States looked upon those declarations.

The legend of the Monroe Doctrine stretching out its wings to protect Latin American independence, should have faded away after the failure of those early attempts by Latin American statesmen to make the Monroe Doctrine the ma-

terial and continent-wide guaranty which they cherished. A brief review of them, and of the manner in which they were received and overcome by the United States, is, therefore, pertinent at this point.

1. Exactly seven months after President Monroe had issued his famous message, Señor Maria Salazar, Colombian Minister to the United States, wrote to Secretary Adams acknowledging the great pleasure with which Colombia had learned "that the government of the United States has undertaken to oppose the policy and the ulterior designs of the Holy Alliance." He added:

In such circumstances, the government of Colombia desires to know *in what manner the government of the United States intends to resist any interference of the Holy Alliance* for the purpose of subjugating the new republics or of interfering with their form of government: Colombia desires to know if the United States will enter into *a treaty of alliance with her to save America from the calamities of a despotic system.*

One month later, August 6, 1824, Secretary Adams replied in unmistakable terms that "by the constitution of the United States, the ultimate decision of this question belongs to the Legislative Department of the Government." He further discouraged the candid hopes of the Colombian Minister:

As however the occasion for this resort could arise only by a deliberate and concerted system of the Allied Powers to exercise force against the freedom and Independence of your Republic; so it is obvious that *the United States could not undertake resistance to them by force of Arms,* without a previous understanding with those European Powers, whose Interests and whose principles would secure from them an active and efficient cooperation in the cause. This there is no reason to doubt could be obtained, but it could only be effected by negotiation *preliminary to that of any alliance between the United States and the Colombian republic,* or in any event coeval with it.

The Secretary of State ended his reply with a re-affirmation of the neutrality which the United States *"have hitherto observed"* in the conflict between Spain and the new republics.

It is not hard to picture the disappointment of the Colombian government, which, only a few weeks before, through Vice-President Santander, had called Monroe's message "an act worthy of the classic land of liberty," "a policy consolatory to the human race," which *"might secure to Colombia a powerful ally in case her independence and liberty should be menaced by the allied powers."*

2. On January 28, 1825, Senhor José Silvestre Rebello, Brazilian Chargé d'affaires in the United States, addressed a long communication to Secretary Adams, in which, after quoting the famous declarations of President Monroe, he pointed to the possibility, although remote at the time, of some European powers helping Portugal in her attempts to recolonize Brazil, and stated very solemnly:

Considering that in such an event *the United States would be bound to put into practice the policy laid down in the said Message,* giving proofs of the generosity and justice which animates her, which could not be done without sacrifice of life and treasure; and it not being in accordance with reason, justice and right that the Government of Brazil should accept such sacrifices gratuitously: that Government *is ready to enter into a Convention with the Government of of the United States,* the object of which

will be the preservation of the Independence of Brazil in the case of any Power aiding Portugal in its vain and chimerical projects for the recolonization of Brazil.

The same reason which moves the Government of Brazil to hope that the Government of the United State will propose the conditions for the said Convention permits it also to hope that the Government of the United States will also offer conditions for entering into *an offensive and defensive alliance with the Government of Brazil.*

This note not having been answered by Adams, who soon afterwards became President of the United States, the Brazilian diplomat insisted on its terms in a later communication addressed to Henry Clay, Adams' successor.

The new Secretary of State replied, on April 13, 1825, disavowing any likelihood of a concerted European aggression against Brazil and declining to enter into the proposed convention for the protection of Brazilian independence. As for the treaty of alliance, which the Brazilian representative suggested as the logical corollary of President Monroe's message, Secretary Clay answered:

But *such a Treaty would be inconsistent with the policy which the United States have heretofore prescribed to themselves.* That policy is, that whilst the war is confined to the parent country and its former Colony, *the United States remain neutral,* extending their friendship and doing equal justice to both parties. From that policy *they did not deviate during the whole of the long contest between Spain and the several Independent Governments* which have been erected on her former American Territories.

This time the disappointment was for the Brazilian Minister of Foreign Affairs, who, in his instructions to the Brazilian Chargé d'affaires at Washington, had interpreted the message of President

Monroe as advising the *"necessity of our combining and standing shoulder to shoulder for the defence of our rights and our territory."*

3. As early as May 3, 1824, the Executive Government of Buenos Aires, in a message to the Legislative Assembly, made reference to the "great principles" announced by President Monroe, and declared that the diplomatic representative of the United Provinces to Washington had been instructed "to suggest to the Government of that Republic how desirable it would be if, *in addition to those two great Principles* . . . it could also be declared that *none of the Governments of this Continent shall alter by force their respective Boundaries* as recognized at the time of their emancipation."

Of course, it was naïve to suppose that the United States government would commit itself to that extent; not, at any rate, at a time when Texas and Cuba constituted the two great ambitions of expansionists in the United States. But, in mentioning that principle, the Buenos Aires government was only endorsing the theories of Bolívar and other founders of the Latin American republics, who had already advanced their doctrine of the *uti-possidetis* and expressed their aims of continental union.

In August 1826, John M. Forbes, Chargé d'affaires of the United States in Buenos Aires, had a conference with the President of the Argentine Republic in which the concern of the United States for the war then raging between Argentina and Brazil was mentioned in the light of the Monroe message. From Forbes' report and from the communication he received soon afterwards from the Argentine Minister of Foreign Affairs,

it may be established that the Buenos Aires government tried to bring its case within the scope of the Monroe Doctrine. It endeavored to secure the cooperation of the United States against the only monarchical government in South America, that of Brazil, which was, besides, likely to be eventually aided by a European power, namely, Portugal.

The Buenos Aires government wanted to know if that of the United States would in any way feel bound by the Monroe message to help Argentina in that *"war of principles,"* and if the aid of a European power to a belligerent American country should be considered contrary to the Monroe Doctrine or not.

The reply of Secretary of State Clay, which came one year and a half later, left no room for doubt. After stressing the fact that the message of President Monroe was called forth by apprehensions which were no longer true, Secretary Clay said with respect to the nature of the policy outlined by President Monroe:

The declaration must be regarded as having been voluntarily made, and *not as conveying any pledge or obligation,* the performance of which foreign nations have a right to demand. When the case shall arrive, if it should ever occur, of such an European interference as the message supposes, and it becomes consequently necessary to decide *whether this country will or will not* engage in war, Congress alone, you well know, is competent, by our Constitution, to decide that question.

In the second part of his note the Secretary of State denied emphatically that the war between the Argentine Republic and the Emperor of Brazil, "even if Portugal and the Brazils had remained united *and the war had been carried on by their joint arms,"* could be conceived as presenting a state of things "bearing the *remotest analogy* to the case which President Monroe's message deprecates." As usual, he ended by remarking that "the general policy of the United States is that of strict and impartial neutrality in reference to all wars of other Powers."

Thus were the "castles in the air" built by the Argentine statesmen around the Monroe message blown away by the cold logic and the self-interestedness of their Northern colleagues, just as those of the Colombian and the Brazilian governments had been before.

4. On March 7, 1825, Joel R. Poinsett was appointed the first United States Minister to Mexico. In the instructions he received from Secretary of State Clay he was directed to bring to the attention of the Mexican government the advantages embodied in the principles announced by President Monroe. Poinsett not only carried out his instructions, but, desirous of gaining completely the confidence and good will of the Mexican authorities, he expressed to the Mexican Secretary of State that the United States had *"openly declared their determination not to permit any other nation to interpose with armed hand between Spain and the Americas."*

On this and other occasions, Minister Poinsett let his oratorical enthusiasm carry him away, with the result that the Mexican government was given the impression that the United States had really pledged itself to protect Latin American independence by the use of force.

When news of Poinsett's over-zealous diplomacy reached Washington, the gentlemen at the Capitol were greatly upset. The House of Representatives passed a resolution asking the President to explain on what authority the Minister to Mexico had made such generous statements. The resolution requested the head of the

Executive to "inform the House *whether the United States have, in any manner, made any pledge to the Governments of Mexico and South America that the United States would not permit the interference of any foreign power with the independence or form of government of those nations;* and, if so, when, in what manner, and to what effect."

This incident gave the United States government an opportunity to lay down, once for all, and in a public document, the views it had been repeating for years in official state papers.

The report prepared by Secretary Clay, dated March 29, 1826, which President Adams hastened to forward to the House, was so clear and so emphatic as to dismiss completely any further question on the matter. Latin American statesmen would have saved themselves much embarrassment if they had kept it in mind when, in later years, they tried, again, to recognize in the Monroe Doctrine attributes of unselfishness and tendencies of continental union which it never had.

The pertinent part of the report read as follows:

The United States have contracted no engagement, nor made any pledge to the Governments of Mexico and South America, or to either of them, *that the United States would not permit the interference of any foreign power with the independence or form of government of those nations,* nor have any instructions been issued authorizing any such engagement or pledge.

All apprehensions of the danger to which Mr. Monroe alludes, of an interference by the allied powers of Europe to introduce their political systems into this hemisphere, have ceased. If, indeed, an attempt by force had been made by allied Europe to subvert the liberties of the southern nations on this continent, and to erect upon the ruins of their free institutions monarchical systems, the people of the United States would have stood pledged, in the opinion of their Executive, *not to any foreign State, but to themselves and to their posterity, by their dearest interests and highest duties,* to resist to the utmost such attempt; and it is to a pledge of that character that Mr. Poinsett alone refers.

Was this not proving beyond all doubt what the Monroe message really was and what it was not? Should not this public and official declaration of the government of the United States have been sufficient to stop the idealistic speculations of the Latin American patriots?

The eyes of, at least, one Latin American statesman were opened by Secretary Clay. When President Victoria of Mexico heard of the debates in the House of Representatives and of Secretary Clay's report, he said, speaking before the Mexican General Assembly:

The memorable promise of President Monroe, contained in his Message of the 2nd of December 1823, *is disclaimed by the present Government of The United States,* which has publicly declared that "they have contracted no Engagement, nor made any Pledges to the Governments of Mexico, and South America, or to either of them, that the United States would not permit the interference of any Foreign Powers with the Independence, or Form of Government of those nations."

It is, indeed, true, that Mr. Clay, Secretary of State, and Author of the Note, appeals to the sympathy of the People of the United States, and to their community of interests with the New Republicks: but it is no less true that *we have no longer any sort of Guarantee or Promise, on the part of that Government, to take a part in the Contest,* if a Third Power should become an Auxiliary of Spain.

President Victoria, of course, was right in his recognition of the true intentions of the United States. But he was wrong in supposing that these had been different under President Monroe. He had misunderstood Monroe's message, as had all his Latin American colleagues.

The irony of the story is that Henry Clay, who, years before, had been the champion of Latin American independence in the United States Congress, the romantic visionary of continental friendship, perhaps the only Northern leader who had originally seen in Monroe's message something else than mere nationalistic policies, should have also been the one called, as Secretary of State, to dispel all hopes of the Monroe Doctrine ever being converted into a continental, disinterested pact.

On January 20, 1824, less than two months after President Monroe uttered his famous declaration, Clay had introduced in the House of Representatives a joint resolution intended to make it "the law of the land." He had asked Congress to go on record as follows:

. . . That the people of these United States would not see, without serious inquietude, *any forcible interposition by the Allied Powers of Europe in behalf of Spain,* to reduce to their former subjection those parts of the continent of America which have proclaimed and established for themselves, respectively, independent Governments, and which have been solemnly recognised by the United States.

This resolution had been defeated, and thus had failed the only attempt ever made to identify the Monroe Doctrine with the national laws of the United States. The Monroe principles had been left to be the personal expressions of a Chief Executive, with no binding force whatever and subject to the varied interpretations of his successors in office—the most curious interpretations, indeed.

Two years later, when Secretary Clay

was confronted with the turmoil aroused in the House by Poinsett's candid assurances to Mexico, he probably thanked Heaven that his 1824 resolution had not passed.

From the evidence disclosed in the preceding pages, it is not difficult to arrive at the conclusion that *the original Monroe Doctrine was a unilateral, egoistic policy, and exclusively of the United States*—the fourth count of this *indictment* of the Monroe Doctrine.[1]

The later history of the Doctrine, and its amazing transfigurations, only corroborate that conclusion. The Monroe Doctrine had been interpreted, stretched, contracted, stated, and restated arbitrarily by officials of the United States. But their ideas on the matter—most varied, often contradicting—always have one thing in common: the recognition of the exclusive right of the United States to pass upon the Doctrine and to apply it at its own discretion.

This will be more evident further on, as we follow the practical use—and the "non-use"—of the Doctrine in its eventful career. But even at the beginning, when all there was of the Monroe Doctrine was the original message of President Monroe, the views of the Anglo-Saxon American statesmen were not different.

The real Monroe Doctrine, the Monroe Doctrine of 1823, was no less one-sided and self-interested than its outgrowth, the modern Monroe Doctrine of Monroe's successors; with the qualification that the latter is in conflict with the sovereignty and self-respect of the Latin

Americans, while the former happened to be in tune with what was then the main aspiration of the young Southern republics. The original Monroe Doctrine, however, was in favor of the Latin American cause only insofar as this coincided with the interests of the United States. When they ceased to coincide, when Latin America sought further commitments, the latter prevailed.

The message of President Monroe gave no pledge of protection. It implied no obligation whatever on the part of the United States. It was not advanced for the benefit of Latin American safety, nor for the glory of Mr. Monroe's memory in the Americas of Latin origin. That is why the early Latin American attempts to make international, defensive compacts out of it failed so pitifully. That is why, in the words of a distinguished Spanish professor, the dialogue sought by those Latin American envoys to Washington was impossible. In place of it, the Saxon-American monologue prevailed throughout.

Not in vain had John Quincy Adams, Monroe's principal adviser, and later his successor in the Presidency, expressed his contempt for the newly born Latin American republics, as early as 1821, in these words:

War and mutual destruction was in every member of their organization, moral, political, and physical. I had little expectation of any beneficial result to this country *from any future connection with them, political or commercial.* We should derive no improvement to our own institutions by any communion with theirs.

The dialogue was foredoomed, even before the utterance of President Monroe gave thought to it in the minds of Latin American statesmen.

---

[1] The three other indictments, described in previous chapters, are: worn out and useless, merits exaggerated, and never intended for the benefit of Latin Americans.—*Ed.*

LUIS QUINTANILLA (1900-   ) is a distinguished
Mexican diplomat. Born in Paris and educated
at the Sorbonne and at the Johns Hopkins University,
where he received a Ph.D., he has served in many
posts, including Moscow, as ambassador. His book
contains a severe indictment of the Monroe Doctrine.
It reflects all the reasons why South Americans
have been hostile to it for more than a century.
Unlike Nerval, Quintanilla believes that at the
beginning the Doctrine was a good policy but
that it was "gradually fashioned into a Machiavellian
policy for intra-Hemisphere consumption" by means
of the various corollaries. Is it possible that such
a Doctrine might have been an instrument for
solidarity in the hemisphere had it taken a different
direction?*

Machiavellian Due to Corollaries

At the time of its enunciation, the
Monroe Doctrine was intended to be,
essentially, a policy toward Europe; not
a policy for the Hemisphere. It was a
toothless warning indeed, but one definitely aimed at Europe. As such, there is
nothing that we can hold against it. To
reject its original intention would be
tantamount to accepting the right of
Europe to meddle with the nations of our
Hemisphere: and that, no Latin American wants.

It is only by virtue of later interpretations—or rather misinterpretations"—
that the momentous Message was gradually fashioned into a Machiavellian policy
for *intra*-Hemisphere consumption. From
a candid but commendable United States
gesture against European interference,
the Doctrine was turned into a ruthless
axiom, utilized by Washington adminis-
trations to suit the interests of what is
known as *"Yankee Imperialism."* Because
the Doctrine—certainly through no fault
of its victims—was perverted to the point
of being invoked as a justification for
attacks against the sovereignty of the
nations which it claimed to protect, it
bulks large today as a stumbling block in
the way of inter-American relations.
"Paramount Interests," "Manifest Destiny," "Big-Stick Policy," "Watchful
Waiting," "Dollar Diplomacy," "Paternalism," "Protectionism"—in short,

* From Luis Quintanilla, *A Latin American Speaks*, pp. 111–130. New York: The Macmillan Company, 1934. Reprinted without footnotes by permission of the author.

"Yankee Imperialism"—those slogans have become irrevocably connected, in the minds of Latin Americans, with the two words, *"Monroe Doctrine."*

Yes, it may be said that historically there are *two* Monroe Doctrines: the one, promulgated by the President; and the other, the distorted Doctrine of the Corollaries. But the authentic one has been pushed into the background. Today people have not in mind the mild offering of the fifth President of the United States, but the subsequent concoction into which entered all the imperialistic ingredients added by more voracious occupants of the White House, among whom Theodore Roosevelt—twenty-sixth President of the United States of America—stands out conspicuously.

"The Monroe Doctrine, first enunciated by President Monroe in 1823," writes Professor [Frederick L.] Schuman, "was a warning to the European powers to keep out of the American Hemisphere and, by implications and successive reinterpretations, an assertion of the hegemony of the United States over the American continents." That is precisely the point! The Doctrine has come to mean "an assertion of the hegemony of the United States over the American continents": a policy of bloody military occupation and outright diplomatic intervention.

Practically any Spanish American could put forward an impressive list of perfectly legitimate reasons why he rejects vehemently the Monroe Doctrine. A striking sample of genuine Latin American attitude in this respect, can be found in Gaston Nerval's book, significantly entitled *Autopsy of the Monroe Doctrine.* . . .

Scores of charges can be leveled at the Monroe Doctrine by a Latin American.

For the sake of clearness, I will limit the counts of my indictment to five:

1. It is *unilateral.*
2. It proved *inefficient.*
3. It was *perverted.*
4. It is *unpopular.*
5. It has become *outmoded.*

1. There can be no argument concerning the first count. Practically all historians, Anglo-Saxon as well as Latin, agree on that. Even Dr. Perkins writes: "The Monroe Doctrine was not, and was not intended to be, anything else than a unilateral declaration of policy. From that day to this American statesmen have insisted upon its purely American character, upon the right of the United States to interpret it in its own fashion, and on the basis of its own interests." . . . The Monroe Doctrine was never meant to be anything but a one-sided policy. To pretend otherwise, is to commit historical heresy. . . .

The Doctrine was a *monologue,* not a dialogue. It assumed, after the Theodore Roosevelt Corollary, an order of things entirely created and maintained by a self-appointed *guardian;* not one agreed to by equal partners. Why speak of "Americanization" or "continentalization"? Whatever rabbits Monroeist magicians pull out of their hats, that thing called Pan Americanism will never come out of it!

The Doctrine was unilateral not only in its proclamation, definition, and application, but also in its original motive, which was not the safety of the Hemisphere, but the security of the United States. So well known an authority as Professor Charles Edward Chapman, states: "The benevolent feature never was, and is not, the primary purpose of the doctrine. Its fundamental idea has always been *the security of the United States*. In this all-important respect, the Monroe Doctrine has not 'changed,' as so often alleged." The security of the United States: again, there is nothing the matter with that. Pan Americanism also includes it—but does not stop there. It cares not only for the security of the United States but for that 'of all and each of the American Republics. *Good-Neighbor Pan Americanism is a joint enterprice freely undertaken by partners with equal rights and mutual obligations.* And that is precisely what the Monroe Doctrine is not!

2. *The Doctrine proved inefficient.* To be accurate, one should say that it was created impotent. It was the expression of a wish: to remove from the Western Hemisphere the threat of European military or political interference. But there was never mention of specific measures to be taken, should that wish go unheeded. Every North American statesman made it clear that the Doctrine never implied the slightest pledge by the United States actually to fight for the sovereignty of any American Republic. The man who as Secretary of State is credited with the drafting of the Message read by President Monroe to Congress—John Quincy Adams—said in a Message to the Senate December 26, 1825, after he had become President of his country: "An agreement between all the parties represented at the meeting that each will guard *by its own means* against the establishment of any future European colony within its border may be found advisable. This was more than two years since announced by my predecessor." It could not be clearer: *"each by its own means."* From the outset and from the lips of the statesmen who played the principal parts in the elaboration of the

Doctrine, the world was advised that it was up to every country by its own means to uphold Monroe's recommendation, with the inference that, should any European nation violate such recommendation, the United States would not consider itself obligated to act; nor, of course, the other American republics. The Monroe Doctrine was too platonic to be effective. . . .

Three major instances are commonly mentioned by those who claim the efficiency of the Monroe Doctrine. One is the French intervention in Mexico, 1861-67. The second is the Venezuelan boundary dispute with Great Britain in 1895. The third is the incident in which Venezuela was involved with Germany, England, and Italy, in 1902.

That the Monroe Doctrine had little or nothing to do with the French abandonment of Emperor Maximilian in Mexico is admitted even by Professor Perkins when he writes: "All these considerations taken together make it clear, as must frankly be admitted, that the Empire of Maximilian might have come to an inglorious end, and the French troops been withdrawn from across the seas without the intervention of the United States." As a matter of fact, in Perkins' more recent book, I was happy to find a statement to the effect that "there is much reason to believe that such an assumption [that had it not been for the position of the United States, new, ambitious enterprises might have been attempted on this side of the Atlantic] is a false one; and that the developments of the period from 1865 to 1895 would not have been materially different if Monroe and his successors had not interposed a veto upon the colonization of the New World, or the subversion of its republican governments." I would be, of course, *the last* to disagree with such a statement.

But, safely backed by Professor [John H.] Latané, I may say that the three instances so popular among the stubborn defenders of the Monroe Doctrine (plus its Corollaries) worked out for the good of the Hemisphere, not because of the Doctrine, but because, Monroe or no Monroe, the European powers involved in Western Hemisphere interventions had to abandon their adventures on account of European conditions involving the problem of European balance of power. Professor Latané maintains that the French (aside from the heroic resistance put up by the thousands of Mexican citizens who died for the freedom of their country, under the leadership of the immortal Juárez) would have been obliged to withdraw all support of the Austrian-born Mexican Emperor because, coincidently with what amounted to an ultimatum from Abraham Lincoln, word had reached Napoleon III of Bismarck's determination to force a war with Austria over the Schleswig-Holstein controversy. "Napoleon realized that the territorial aggrandizement of Prussia . . . would be a serious blow to his prestige and in fact endanger his throne . . . in order to have a free hand to meet the European situation he decided to yield to the American demands. As the European situation developed he hastened the final withdrawal of his troops and left Maximilian to his fate. . . . Thus," Professor Latané concludes ironically, "the Monroe Doctrine was vindicated."

As is well known, the dispute of 1895 originated from the conflicting contentions of Venezuela and Great Britain on 30,000 square miles of territory on the border of the South American republic and British Guiana. In a message to Congress, President Cleveland declared that the acquisition of territory, in America, by a European power, was a clear violation of the Monroe Doctrine; and he asked Congress to take steps for the appointment of a commission to determine the true boundary. "Here was a bold and unqualified defiance of England. No one before had ever trod so roughly on the British lion's tail with impunity. The English-speaking public on both sides of the Atlantic was stunned and amazed. . . . But here again," writes Latané, "the true explanation is to be found in events that were happening in another quarter of the globe." Cleveland's Venezuelan Message was sent to Congress on December 17th. At the end of the year came Dr. Jameson's raid into the Transvaal, and on the 3rd of January the German Kaiser sent his famous telegram of congratulation to Paul Kruger. The wrath of England was suddenly diverted from America to Germany, and Lord Salisbury avoided a rupture with the United States over a matter which after all was not of such serious moment to England in order to be free to deal with a question involving much greater interests in South Africa. The Monroe Doctrine was none the less effectively vindicated." . . .

3. *The Doctrine was perverted.* Originally it meant, "America not for Europe," but the Corollaries made it say, "America for the U.S.A." Cuba, Puerto Rico, Panama, the Dominican Republic, Haiti, Nicaragua—six United States "protectorates" in less than fifteen years. Outright interventions, with Marines landing, occupying territories, setting up governments and running the country: in Cuba from 1898 to 1903, then from 1906 to 1909, again in 1912, and finally from 1917 to 1922; in the Dominican Re-

public, from 1916 to 1924; in Nicaragua, from 1912 to 1933, practically without interruption; in Haiti, from 1915 to 1934. We can mention these facts because they represent a policy which belongs to the past. We *must* mention them because, since they cannot be forgotten, we expect the United States at least to admit them and never to minimize their historical significance. Wrongs belong to the past only when you are able to talk about them and still be friends.

That is precisely our attitude today: do not keep wrongs bottled up inside. Friendship is a positive, driving force. Frustrated rancor cannot be taken for love. Not to fear is necessary but not sufficient. Friendship is not restraint but forward impulse.

The Monroe Doctrine is guilty—not only because it did not prevent but because it even was invoked to justify manifestations of imperialism. Rather, not the original Message, but its inglorious additions. There are a good many Corollaries. I will mention the most significant ones:

In 1825, Secretary of State Clay declared that the United States could not consent to the occupation of Cuba and Puerto Rico, by "any other power than Spain." The idea was good, as is often the case in the history of Monroe's Problem Doctrine. It is better known today as the "No transfer" principle, reiterated by Van Buren in 1829, Forsyth in 1840, Webster in 1843, and consecrated at the Habana 1940 Conference. Yet the timely warning did not apply to the United States, which, for too many years, made of Cuba a virtual Protectorate. Until 1936, when Franklin D. Roosevelt's Administration renounced the right of intervention granted to its country by the well known Platt Amendment, Cuba

was freed from Spain but remained subjugated to the U.S.A.

In 1845, President Polk—of whom Abraham Lincoln said, "He feels the blood of this [Mexican] war, like the blood of Abel crying to heaven against him"—added his Corollary, intended to justify the annexation of Texas. Said he: "We can never consent that European powers shall interfere to prevent such a union [of Texas and the United States] because it might disturb the 'balance of power,' which they [European countries] may desire to maintain upon this continent." So, having promulgated the Doctrine to redress and maintain the balance of power *in Europe,* a North American President claimed that Europe, in turn, had no right to be concerned over changes in the balance of power of the Western Hemisphere.

The second of the so-called "Grant Corollaries," in 1871 conceded the Dominican Republic the right to annex itself to the United States. President Grant stated: "I believe . . . that *our institutions were broad enough to extend over the entire continent* as rapidly as other peoples might desire to bring themselves under our protection. . . . In view of the facts which had been laid before me, and *with an earnest desire to maintain the 'Monroe Doctrine,'* I believed that I would be derelict in my duty if I did not take measures" in regard to the annexation of the Republic of Santo Domingo.

Under President Cleveland . . . in 1895, came the arrogant Olney Corollary, added by that Secretary of State who shouted to the world: "Today the United States *is practically sovereign on this continent and its fiat is law* upon the subjects to which it confines its interposition . . . its infinite resources combined with its isolated position render it *master of the situation* and practically invulnerable as against any or all other powers. . . ." It is recorded in history, as "Olney's Fiat." The word of the United States was to be a command, not only to European meddlers but to the "subjects" of Latin America's protectorates—and this bombastic attitude was based on the fact that "its infinite resources combined with its isolated position render it *master of the situation* and practically invulnerable as against any or all other powers!" How foolish it all sounds today! Nothing could be more opposed to contemporary Pan Americanism, nothing less acceptable to Latin America. Olney's Fiat was a new expression of United States hegemony. So was the well known Theodore Roosevelt addition: the famous Roosevelt Corollary which dealt the Doctrine its death blow.

On December 6, 1904, "Big Stick" T. R. solemnly declared: "Any country whose people conduct themselves well, can count upon our hearty friendship. If a nation shows that it knows how to act with reasonable efficiency and decency in social and political matters, if it keeps order and pays its obligations, it need fear no interference from the United States. Chronic wrongdoing or an impotence which results in a general loosening of the ties of civilized society, may in America, as elsewhere, ultimately require intervention by some civilized nation, and in the Western Hemisphere the adherence of the United States to the Monroe Doctrine may force the United States, however reluctantly, in flagrant cases of such wrongdoing or impotence, to the exercise of an international power."

No document has proved more harmful to the prestige of the United States in the Western Hemisphere. No White House policy could be more distasteful to Latin Americans—not even, perhaps, outspoken imperialism. Latin Americans are usually inclined to admire strength, force, a nation *muy hombre*. This was imperialism without military glamour: this was imperialism *à la* Tartufe, not even *à la* Napoléon. Moreover, it was a total distortion of the original Message. Monroe's Doctrine was defensive and negative: defensive, in that it was essentially an opposition to eventual aggression from Europe; negative, in that it simply told Europe what it *should not* do—not what the United States *should* do. The Monroe Doctrine of later Corollaries became aggressive and positive: aggressive, because even without actual European attack, it urged United States "protection" of Latin America—and that was outright intervention; positive, because instead of telling Europe what *not* to do, it told the United States what it *should* do in the Western Hemisphere. From a case of America *vs.* Europe, the Corollaries made of the Doctrine a case of United States *vs.* America. President Monroe had merely shaken his head, brandished his finger, and said to Europe, "Now, now, gentlemen, if you meddle with us, we will not love you any more," while Teddy Roosevelt, brandishing a big stick, had shouted, "Listen, you guys, don't muscle in—this territory is ours."

In still another Corollary, enunciated to justify United States intervention, the same Roosevelt said: "It is far better that this country should put through such an arrangement [enforcing fulfillment of financial obligations contracted by Latin American states] rather than to allow any foreign country to undertake it." To intervene in order to protect: to intervene, in order to prevent others from so doing. It is the "Invasion for Protection" corollary, so much in the limelight recently, in other parts of the world.

4. Thus, in the light of historical facts —laying aside considerations of theoretical value—one can easily understand why the Monroe Doctrine became so *unpopular* not only among Latin Americans but also among an increasing number of people of the United States. Those who do not yet see the point would do well to put themselves, by a stretch of the imagination, in the victims' shoes. Latin Americans . . . are just as patriotic and liberty-loving as Anglo-Americans. Unless you begin your analysis on that assumption, you are not qualified to judge the problem of inter-Americanism. Latin Americans, even those who admire the technical superiority of their powerful industrial neighbor, do not recognize the political or moral tutelage of the United States. We have seen that some Latin American countries are ahead of the United States in social legislation. Mexico's agrarian policy, for instance, is certainly more advanced than that of the United States. I could name many other important fields in which Latin America maintains a moral leadership. But one should avoid unnecessary comparisons. It is enough to proclaim that Latin Americans love "life, liberty, and the pursuit of happiness" as ardently as their northern neighbors. So, any reminder directly or indirectly connected with brutal attacks from without, whoever the aggressor, automatically revives legitimate Latin American resentment.

Many authorized spokesmen of public opinion in the United States have been as frank as Latin American critics. On December 28, 1933, President Roosevelt, commemorating the birthday of Woodrow Wilson, admitted: "I do not hesitate to say that if I had been engaged in a political campaign as a citizen of some other American republic I might have been strongly tempted to play upon the fears of my compatriots of that republic by charging the United States of North America with some form of imperialistic desire for selfish aggrandizement."

Also referring to those dark years of inter-American relations, a distinguished United States authority on Latin America, Professor [J. Fred] Rippy of Duke University wrote: "It is in vain that we plead our innocence of imperialism. Our whole history gives a lie to such a plea . . . A policy which has brought under our virtual domination some nine to twelve republics in a generation, may differ from European imperialism in form; but it is very near that imperialism, in substance." And a recent well known interpreter of Hemisphere conditions wrote in even stronger words: "In the past whenever we wanted territory we took it. We took Texas, New Mexico, and California from Mexico. We took Cuba from Spain. We took Panama from Colombia. And we were more forthright than the German, Italian, or Japanese aggressors. 'I took the Canal Zone,' said Theodore Roosevelt bluntly. We were equally forthright about landing the United States Marines to defend the property of banking and fruit companies in what we contemptuously referred to as 'banana republics.' And at one moment North American officials directed the financial policies of eleven of the twenty Latin American countries, while in six these banking agents were backed by American bayonets on the spot. In our conquests and in our interventions we frequently cited the Monroe Doctrine."

The Monroe Doctrine, with its imperialistic connotations, is loaded with the kind of explosive that endangers the Pan

American structure. That explains why United States Presidents sincerely concerned with their neighbors' feelings, from Abraham Lincoln to Franklin D. Roosevelt, have found no need to mention the Monroe Doctrine. Not even during the meeting of foreign ministers of the Americas, held at Rio de Janeiro in January, 1942, did the skillful United States delegate, Sumner Welles, mention the name of that unhappy Doctrine which for the last fifty years has been the greatest stumbling block in the way of genuine inter-Americanism. And there is no doubt that the situation discussed at the Rio Conference was one which, had the Message of 1823 not been perverted, would have fallen within the jurisdiction of the original Doctrine. But, right or wrong, the delegates knew that the emotional connotations of the words "Monroe Doctrine" were such that they could not be pronounced without stirring up legitimate ill fellings. *The moment Monroe's distorted shadow enters a Pan American Conference, the Good Neighbors disband.* The silence made around the Monroe Doctrine at the historical meeting at Rio is more eloquent than any indictment ever uttered against it.

5. Finally . . . it is obvious that the Doctrine seems completely *outmoded.* The days in which a single country—however powerful—could claim the exclusive right to behave, on the world stage, as a "rugged individualist," are gone forever. Ask Napoleon, ask the Kaiser, or ask Hitler! Civilized order is a joint enterprise, freely accepted by all partners. Mankind does not allow gangsters, be they individuals or nations. Order was established, first among the members of the family, then among the residents of the community, later among the citizens of a nation. Finally the day is near when a cooperative international order will be established among the nations of the earth. That order, whether local or national, continental or international, can be conceived only as a joint enterprise. America was the first continent in history to struggle for the establishment of such order. There can be no room in this continent for a doctrine which, even at its best and in its original intention, rests essentially on the arbitrary decision of one self-appointed "leader." The hour of selfish nationalism is past. There is no room for anarchy in organized society. Because the welfare of the many must prevail over that of the few, Monroeist Pan Americanism has been gradually but irrevocably displaced by democratic Pan Americanism.

The Monroe Doctrine may not be dead, but there is little use for it today. And there certainly will be less room for it in the world of tomorrow.

International Affairs is a Soviet periodical founded in 1954, published in Moscow, and printed in Russian, English, and French. It is called a monthly journal of political analysis and is published by the Soviet Society for the Popularization of Political and Scientific Knowledge. S. GONIONSKY, an apparently obscure journalist (his name does not appear in any list of Soviet writers), contends that the Monroe Doctrine's original purpose was to give the United States exclusive rights to exploit Latin America. After describing the various instances of American penetration under the cloak of the Doctrine since 1823, he concludes that because of the recent overthrow of American stooges in some of the republics, Yankee interventions will cease and the Doctrine will be useless.*

Imperialistic and Now Outdated

American diplomacy has long been renowned for its inexhaustible ingenuity in devising all sorts of "doctrines." Most of them, it is true, fade into oblivion as soon as they appear giving way to fresh and just as short-lived official definitions of U.S. foreign policy "principles."

But Washington diplomats have a "doctrine" that is 137 years old and not forgotten yet, although in fact, it is dead, because the situation in which it originated has long since changed. It is the Monroe Doctrine. The State Department stubbornly refuses to inter its corpse and even goes so far as to maintain that it is not a corpse at all. Washington tries to galvanize it, falling back upon Monroe's formulas in "justifying" the present foreign policy of the United States—one that accords just as little with the present international scene as the Monroe Doctrine itself.

The latest effort to galvanize the Monroe Doctrine was made by the Department of State on July 14, 1960. Washington's diplomats claim in a blustering and unsubstantiated statement that "the principles of the Monroe Doctrine are as valid today as they were in 1823 when the Doctrine was proclaimed," and that "these principles are not professed by itself alone [i.e., by Washington.—S.G.], but represent through solemn agreements the views of the

* S. Gonionsky, "The Unburied Corpse of the Monroe Doctrine," *International Affairs,* October 1960, pp. 60-66.

American community as a whole." In other words, the top men in Herter's[1] department maintain that the Monroe Doctrine, which is ultimately directed against the independence of the Latin American countries and personifies the policy which has turned the latter into semi-colonies of the United States, is now hailed and supported by those selfsame countries.

Needless to say, the State Department claim is false from start to finish. This is amply demonstrated by the application of the Monroe Doctrine throughout its history, and in particular by the "solemn agreements" imposed by the U.S.A. on the members of the "American community," i.e., the Governments of the Latin American countries. Let us examine the facts and pertinent documents. To begin with, let us look at President James Monroe's message to Congress of December 2, 1823.

The United States, wrote President Monroe, declares that the American continents are "henceforth not to be considered as subjects for future colonization by any European Power" and that the United States considers any attempt on the part of the European Powers "to extend their system to any portion of this hemisphere as dangerous to our peace and safety."

While declaring that the United States would not interfere in European affairs and with the colonies of the European Powers in America, the message went on to say:

"But with the Governments [of American states.—S.G.] who have declared their independence and maintained it, and whose independence we have . . . acknowledged, we could not view any interposition . . . by any European Power

[1] U.S. Secretary of State.—Ed.

in any other light than as the manifestation of an unfriendly disposition toward the United States."

Thus, Washington posed as an opponent of the avowed intention of the European Powers to suppress the national-liberation movement in the Spanish and Portuguese colonies of South and Central America. It acted against the French intentions of exploiting that movement to turn the Spanish colonies into French ones, and against British ambitions to dominate the new American states burgeoning in place of the liberated colonies. Last but not least, the United States feared that tsarist Russia, which then had colonies in North America (Alaska), would try to extend them, and it was determined to defeat Russia's plans.

Viewed from that angle, the Monroe Doctrine was defensive and in a way even progressive, in character (inasmuch as the foreign policy of the European Powers was an incarnation of the darkest semi-feudal reaction). But the defensive aspect of the doctrine was unessential, since the European designs listed above (with the possible exception of the British) were scarcely feasible. The main purpose behind Washington's move was to proclaim the exclusive "right" of the United States to interfere in the affairs of any country in the Western Hemisphere, and to do so under the pretext of protecting the independance of the newly established Latin American states. It was not to prevent European expansion, but rather to facilitate the United States expansion throughout the whole of America, that was the guiding motive behind the Monroe Doctrine.

These very same Spanish possessions in the Western Hemisphere, for which

President Monroe showed such touching "concern," have been the key objects of U.S. predatory ambitions years before 1823. As far back as 1786, one of the makers of U.S. foreign policy, Thomas Jefferson, defined the objectives of his country's ruling element in the following way:

"Our confederacy must be viewed as the nest from which all America, North and South, is to be peopled. We should take care too not to think it for the interest of that great continent to press too soon on the Spaniards. Those countries [the Spanish colonies in America. —S.G.] cannot be in better hands. My fear is that they [the Spaniards.—S.G.] are too feeble to hold them till our population can be sufficiently advanced to gain it [the continent.—S.G.] from them piece by piece." Even Jefferson, as you see, whose name is associated with a number of democratic measures at home, favoured seizure of foreign territories.

In 1803, the United States took advantage of the fact that the British and French were embroiled in the Anglo-French war and closed a deal with Napoleon, "buying" Spanish Louisiana which did not belong to France, from him. In 1810-1812, the United States again profited by the wars in Europe to seize western Florida under the pretext that the Spanish possessions in America had become a seat of the "dangerous ideas" of the French Revolution, coming from Europe. In 1818, U.S. troops followed this up by seizing eastern Florida under the pretext of combatting "Indian raids" and these selfsame "dangerous ideas."

It should be noted that Jefferson directly advised President Washington to adopt the following tactics in making seizures of that sort. "I wish a hundred thousand of our inhabitants would accept the invitation [the reference is to a statement of the Spanish Governor of Eastern Florida, Quesada, who invited foreigners to settle there.—S.G.]. It may be the means of delivering to us peacefully what may otherwise cost a war." It was as early as the late 18th century that the United States took note of the possibilities of so-called "peaceful" annexations of foreign territories—later typical of U.S. methods of expansion.

It is interesting that while it seized one Spanish possession after another, the United States assured Spain of its most friendly sentiments, "guaranteed" her peace and "the strictest neutrality," and promised American assistance and good will. In his *Notes on Imperialism,* V. I. Lenin made the following comment concerning America's hypocrisy in seizing Florida, "Not bad! ('Alliance'—and 'sale')."

American history books still make free with the claim that the United States was well disposed to the struggle of the insurgents in the Spanish colonies. Yet the notorious "neutrality" which the United States proclaimed in the late 18th century was hostile to the independence of the Latin American countries. Under cover of "non-interference," the United States supplied Spanish troops in America with food and munitions, and refused the same to the insurgent Latin American juntas. Indeed, in pursuance of its masked intervention, it sought to stamp out the liberation movement through the Spanish royalists and colonialists, and its own agents.

In spite of this, it had become clear by 1822 that the days of the Spanish monarchy in Latin America were numbered, and that the independence of the new Latin American states was a matter of months. It was only at this point that the United States took account of the failure of its interventionist designs, tried to grab the lion's share of Latin American commerce and sought to win new territorial concessions by declaring that "the American provinces of Spain, which have declared their independence, and are in the enjoyment of it, ought to be recognized by the United States as independent nations."

But while recognizing their independence from Spain, Washington sought to make them dependent upon the United States, and, in the final analysis, to establish an "American political system," i.e., to build up its colonial empire of nominally sovereign Latin American countries weakened by the prolonged wars of liberation. It was this programme for the establishment of the "American political system" in the Western Hemisphere that was rounded out by the Monroe Doctrine, which consummated the aggressive and two-faced policy of the North American colonialists towards their neighbours in the South. It also ushered in a new phase in the development of the Latin American policy of the United States, the phase of intensified U.S. expansion.

In this new phase Washington continued to pose as the defender of the young Latin American republics from the predatory ambitions of the European colonial Powers. But history shows that whenever these countries really did need protection, the United States, far from providing it, frequently assisted the European colonialists. Here are a few examples.

In 1829, a Spanish army of 4,000 attacked Mexico from Cuba. The United States preferred "not to notice" this fact. In 1883, Britain seized the Malvinas

(now Falklands) from the Argentine with U.S. help. In 1835, the United States refused support to the resistance put up by the Central American states against part of the Honduras being turned into a British colony. In 1837, the British navy blockaded Cartagena in Colombia, and in 1838, a French squadron blockaded the Mexican port of Vera Cruz. In both cases, the United States showed no inclination whatever to oppose these acts.

In 1847, the British made a landing in Nicaragua, and established a protectorate —the Mosquito Coast. In 1848, abetted by the United States, Britain extended the frontiers of British Guiana at the expense of Venezuela. In 1852, Britain founded a new colony in the Caribbean Sea, composed of the Bay Islands which belonged to Honduras. In 1861, Spain restored her rule in Santo Domingo, and that same year a French expeditionary corps established a monarchy in Mexico. In 1864, a Spanish flotilla captured the Peru islands of Chincha. In all these cases, the United States made no move to check the British, French, and Spanish colonialists, although the spirit and letter of the Monroe Doctrine prescribed it to do so.

Within a few years after proclaiming the Monroe Doctrine, the United States officially tried to evade the responsibilities following from that doctrine whenever this went against its interests.

In 1825, for example, the Brazilian Government proposed to the United States to conclude a defensive pact guaranteeing Brazil's independence in the event Portugal were to attack her with the support of other European Powers to restore Portuguese rule in that former colony. U.S. State Secretary Henry Clay refused, claiming that a pact of that kind did not accrue from the Monroe Doctrine, although, in substance, Brazil only wanted what was virtually a confirmation of the avowed principle of Washington's foreign policy as formulated in President Monroe's message.

At the same time, the United States tried to extend the sphere of its own colonialist "political system," on more than one occasion taking advantage of the situation created in Latin America by the aggressive acts of the European Powers.

The very next year after proclaiming the Monroe Doctrine, U.S. ruling elements gave a graphic demonstration of its true purpose by landing troops in Puerto Rico. In 1831, U.S. marines landed on the Malvina Islands, and four years later in Peru. In 1846, the United States saddled the viceroyalty of New Granada (later Colombia) with an "agreement" which gave it control over the Isthmus of Panama, part of the viceroyalty. From 1846 to 1848, the United States waged an aggressive war against Mexico, annexing nearly half of Mexico's territory.

In the subsequent period, the United States landed its troops in the Argentine (1852-1853 and 1890), Nicaragua (1853-1854, 1857, 1894), Uruguay (1855 and 1858), Colombia (1856, 1865, 1885), Paraguay (1859), again in Mexico (1873-1882), Chile (1891), and Brazil (1893-1894).

. The insolence of American imperialism grew apace with the growth of its economic and military power. In 1898, the United States waged a successful war against Spain, seizing the Philippines, Guam and, in effect, Cuba. It compelled Spain to relinquish its rights to Puerto Rico. What is more, in 1901, Washington bullied Cuba into inserting the so-called "amendment" of U.S. Senator Platt into the Cuban Constitution, which turned the Cuban Republic, freshly liberated from Spanish rule and only just proclaimed independent, into a virtual colony of the United States.

In the 20th century, U.S. expansion in Latin America gained in scope, but its methods were modified to some extent. Open intervention alternated with the organization of *coups d'état*. But every time, whatever the method, the affair culminated in the placement of Washington's *protégé* at the helm and the entrenchment of North American capital in the country concerned. Here is the far from complete list of U.S. armed interventions in Latin American countries between 1904 and 1917:

Dominican Republic—1904 and 1916; Cuba—1906, 1912 and 1917; Honduras —1907 and 1912; Nicaragua—1909 and 1912; Haiti—1914 and 1915; Mexico— 1914 and 1916, (etc., etc.).

The conclusion is self-evident. The Monroe Doctrine has never had anything in common with the interests of the Latin American countries, and has always been an instrument of oppression, plunder, and enslavement of Latin Americans. It is only natural that it has never been recognized in any of the Latin American countries, nor, for that matter, in any of the European countries, either at the time when it was proclaimed or at any later date. Even in the United States, Congress practically refused it legislative recognition by not adopting any resolution concerning the "principles" of foreign policy formulated in President Monroe's message. It would be so much labour lost to look for any endorsement of these "principles" in any international acts, and the recent attempts of the U.S. Government to assert the reverse are obviously meant to mislead public opinion.

Simon Bolivar, Jose de San Martín,

and other outstanding fighters for the independence of Latin American countries grasped the aggressive nature of the Monroe Doctrine from the first. As early as the beginning of the 19th century, the Latin American countries sought safety in numbers against the aggressive policy of the United States, clearly aware of the threat to their independence contained in the "doctrine" that "substantiated" that policy.

These sentiments came to the fore at the congress of Latin American countries convened in Panama by Bolivar in 1826. The contemporary apologists of North American imperalism go out of their way to represent Bolivar as the father of pan-Americanism, i.e., of a political alliance of all American countries under the leadership of the United States. But in reality, he voiced the interests and sentiments of the peoples of Latin America, who were highly suspicious of the U.S.A. Bolivar was inclined to see only spokesmen of the Latin American republics at the congress, and to have it form a confederation for the purpose of jointly defending their independence against any possible enemy.

True, the confederation idea fell through. But by initiating a movement of the Latin American peoples for unity and defence of their independence, the Panama congress, in effect, condemned the Monroe Doctrine three years after it was proclaimed. The doctrine discredited itself entirely in the 19th century. All the more today, as N. S. Khrushchov pointed out, it has "outlived its time, has come to nought, and has, so to say, died a natural death."

But the United States is stubbornly persisting in its colonialist policy in Latin America, for whose "substantiation" the Monroe Doctrine was proclaimed in the past. That is why Washington is so insistent in stressing the validity of that "doctrine," which has discredited itself over and over again. In the imperialist period it has even been supplemented by overweening official comments, which only served to emphasize its aggressive character. But at the same time, the U.S.A. has engaged in demagogy to enlist support for the political programme of the Monroe Doctrine among the ruling classes and governing cliques in the Latin American countries.

The task facing Washington diplomats has been made easier by the economic backwardness of these countries (originating primarily from the policy of the North American and European colonialists), their great dependence upon the U.S. market, the venality of their semi-feudal landlords and an appreciable section of the bourgeoisie and the military and civil bureaucracy of the Latin American states that has sprung from their midst, and, last but not least, by the efforts of the spiderweb of U.S. agents. To counteract the liberation movement of the Latin American nations, aimed against the United States, the latter succeeded at the close of the 19th century in establishing a Pan-American Union of governing cliques under the leadership of the United States.

The first Pan-American Conference was held in Washington in 1889-1890. The Commercial Bureau of the American Republics was set up at the conference, and Washington proceeded forthwith to turn that commercial body into a military and political bloc of countries of the Western Hemisphere under the aegis of the United States. Ever since then the term Pan-Americanism has become common usage. It was called upon to back the myth that relations between the United States and the Latin American countries would from then on develop on a basis of equality. It was meant to create the impression that the policy formulated in the Monroe Doctrine would no longer be the unilateral line of the United States, but would be regulated by the collective will of all the members of the Pan-American Union.

But, of course, nothing had really changed. Indeed, as the prominent progressive Uruguayan leader, Arismendi, wrote, "only charlatans, unprincipled intriguers, opportunists and chameleons of the political world would maintain unblushingly that a crippled Indian or Latin American creole has common interests with the owners of bottomless safes in Wall Street and the Park Avenue millionaires."

Moreover, official Washington comments appearing five years after the first Pan-American Conference, shattered all possible illusions on that score, demonstrating beyond all doubt that the United States still considered its arbitrary rule the ultimate law in Latin America.

"Today," wrote State Secretary Richard Olney in 1895, "the United States is practically sovereign on this [the American.—S.G.] continent, and its fiat is law upon the subjects to which it confines its interposition." An even more candid interpretation of the Monroe Doctrine was produced by President Theodore Roosevelt, who declared in a message to Congress in 1904 that the adherence to it "may force the United States . . . to the exercise of an international police power," meaning that it was not merely entitled, but obliged, to systematically intervene militarily in Latin America in collecting debts and introducing "law and order." Parker Moon, the American

historian, had every reason to say, as he did, that Theodore Roosevelt had thus turned the Monroe Doctrine into a mandate for North American imperialism.

In the 1920s, the prominent Argentine lawyer, Quintana, characterizing U.S. foreign policy, wrote: "The Monroe Doctrine is not a doctrine of 'America for the Americans,' but of 'America for the North Americans.' . . ." It "has served as an admirable instrument for the United States to separate Europe from America and to establish its hegemony over the latter. The United States has been at all times preoccupied in obtaining concessions of every kind at the cost of the sovereignty of the rest of the American states." He wrote that "the doctrine was dangerous because it was North American imperialism hidden under a principle of international law."

This description of the Monroe Doctrine was reiterated in substance by U.S. State Secretary Charles Evans Hughes in 1923, on the doctrine's 100th anniversary.

He said in part: "So far as the region of the Caribbean Sea is concerned, it may be said that if we had no Monroe Doctrine we should have to create one." In other words, the Caribbean countries belonged to the United States and President Monroe had been wise to supply Washington in good time with a doctrine ideologically "substantiating" the sacred right of the North American monopolies to do what they wished in that area.

It strikes one that similar declarations of U.S. statesmen date back to the turn of the century until the 1930s. This was the time when the United States not only entered the imperialist period but when North American imperialism became the leading force in the capitalist camp. Those were the years when Washington and Wall Street felt for the first time that the situation had at last become propitious for the complete realization of President Monroe's programme, which demanded that other big Powers should not obstruct the United States in doing whatever it wished in both Americas. The only force which could have withstood the United States in the Western Hemisphere—the national-liberation movement of the peoples of Latin America—was not powerful and organized enough as yet to do so, and the U.S.-imposed Pan-Americanism was in some measure stunting its development.

Such were the conditions in which outright violence was in effect the sole content of U.S. policy in Latin America, particularly in the Caribbean area, and the marine corps its chief, if not sole, weapon. "I spent most of my time being a high-class muscle man for Big Business, for Wall Street," recollects Smedley Butler, a marine corps general.

"Thus," he continues, "I helped make Mexico and especially Tampico safe for the American oil interests in 1914. I helped make Haiti and Cuba a decent place for the National City Bank to collect revenues in. I helped purify Nicaragua for the international banking house of Brown Brothers in 1909-1912. I brought light to the Dominican Republic for American sugar interests in 1916. I helped make Honduras 'right' for the American fruit companies in 1903."

The policy of open intervention and gross interference in the domestic affairs of the Latin American countries caused widespread discontent. Its continuation involved an increasing danger for U.S. finance capital. The general hatred of Yankees enabled the imperialist rivals of the United States to expand their economic influence in South and Central America. In 1930, the State Department

saw fit to publish the Clark Memorandum (known by the name of an Under-Secretary of State), in which it tried to whitewash U.S. policy and hinted at its possible modification. A few years later, Washington proclaimed the "good-neighbour" policy, which was meant to salvage the Monroe Doctrine programme and enable the U.S.A. to carry it on under a new signboard and by more pliable methods.

The Second World War caused far-reaching changes in the Latin American countries. All of them depend greatly on foreign trade. Yet the war severed their contacts with the European markets, and compelled them to rely in an even greater degree than before on the U.S. market. This reinforced the position of Yankee imperialism in the Western Hemisphere. During the war the United States also succeeded to a certain extent in turning the Latin American countries into its military and strategic bridgehead. It established numerous military, naval, and air bases throughout Latin America.

After the war, the number of bases was augmented, and, moreover, Washington saddled some of the Latin American countries with bilateral military agreements. The so-called Western Hemisphere Defence Treaty, signed in Rio de Janeiro in 1947, hitched the southern neighbours of the United States still tighter to the military chariot of North American imperialism.

While making no formal move to abandon its "good-neighbour" policy, Washington brought obedient Governments, usually headed by reactionary dictator generals, to power in one Latin American country after another. It did so by means of diplomatic or economic pressure, or *Putsches* organized by its agents. The scale of its efforts is well illustrated by the number of *Putsches.* In eight years (1945 to 1953) U.S. agents plotted and provoked *coups d'etat* in Venezuela (1945), Ecuador (1946), Chile (treason of Gonzales Videla in 1947), Costa Rica (1948), Peru (1948), again in Venezuela (1948), Colombia (1949), Bolivia (1951), Cuba (1952), and again in Colombia (1953).

All this hardly differed from the "feats" of the U.S. marine corps in the earlier periods. Washington went out of its way to carry on with the Monroe Doctrine, although ever since the 1930s it avoided making reference to it.

In 1948, at the Bogota conference, the Pan-American system was streamlined, the Pan-American Union being replaced by the Organization of American States. It was a purely demagogic measure of the U.S. Government. Washington described the Organization of American States as the embodiment of the ideas of Simon Bolivar (!). In fact, however, it embodied the doubtful "ideas" of Dulles and the political blindness of Washington, which still hoped to mislead public opinion in Latin America and thus gain a free hand in following the Monroe "principles" as before in its relations with the Latin Americans. Dulles went so far as to try and revive the tradition of direct reference to the Monroe Doctrine. He only modified it slightly. Whereas Monroe tried to "substantiate" the policy of converting the Latin American countries into semi-colonies of the United States by references to the need to protect them from encroachments of European colonialists, Dulles sought to justify the same policy by referring to the "Communist threat" emanating from the Eastern Hemisphere.

In March 1954, Washington diplomats applied pressure and threats to make the Inter-American Conference in Caracas adopt the so-called anti-Communist resolution. The declaration, Dulles stated, "makes as the international policy of this hemisphere [the United States tries to pass off its imperialist policy as the policy of the entire hemisphere.—*S.G.*] a portion of the Monroe Doctrine which has largely been forgotten." The U.S.A. did its best to remind the world about it in June of that same year when the Eisenhower Government organized armed intervention against Guatemala. Today, in the name of that same Monroe Doctrine, the United States is eager to employ its Guatemalan tactics in crushing the Cuban revolution.

But today the situation in Latin America is no longer what it was in the time of Monroe, Olney, Theodore Roosevelt, or General Butler. It even changed sharply since 1954, when the Governments in many Latin American countries were headed by direct U.S. stooges. The mounting national-liberation movement overthrew the sanguinary dictatorship of Rojas Pinilla in Colombia, and then the dictatorships of Pérez Jiménez in Venezuela and Batista in Cuba. Little Cuba has delivered telling blows to Yankee imperialism. The United States is having increasing difficulties in keeping its southern neighbours in check. From a reserve of imperialism, Latin America is steadily turning into a real and active force fighting for peace, national independence, democracy, and progress.

The Monroe "principles" have long since fallen out with the true correlation of forces in the Western Hemisphere. The policy based on the Monroe Doctrine has long since collapsed. But until recently its collapse has been internal and concealed. The vast material resources accumulated by the United States, its military potential, its influence in the capitalist world and its weight on the world market are still saving the day for it. But the intrinsic bankruptcy of its foreign policy in general and in the Western Hemisphere in particular is coming to the surface in increasingly bolder relief.

A profound crisis is shaping in the relations between the U.S.A. and the Latin American countries. This has been brought out, to all intents and purposes, in the recent irritated and absolutely senseless utterances of U.S. statesmen, which boil down to the contention that the Monroe Doctrine "entitles" the U.S.A. to suppress the Cuban revolution. That doctrine is today nothing more than an unburied corpse.

"No matter how many 'doctrines' the ruling circles in America invent or dig out of the dust of history," says the TASS statement of July 16 last, "no one recognizes their right to do what they please with the fate of other nations. Every nation has the right to be master of its own fate, to choose the way of life that responds to its interests, and to dispose of its country's wealth."

Cuban Prime Minister Fidel Castro described the official U.S. references to the Monroe Doctrine as an "insult to the peoples of Latin America." But if the United States proclaims the Monroe Doctrine," he added, "we proclaim our own doctrine of freedom for the peoples of Latin America."

A wind of change is blowing across Latin America.

Long a professor of public law, one of Franklin D. Roosevelt's earliest "brain trusters," and since 1937 a contributing editor of *Newsweek*, RAYMOND MOLEY (1886-   ) replies to both Quintanilla and Gonionsky. For him, the Doctrine is neither outmoded nor dead but relevant and very much alive. The extension of "the political system" of the Soviet Union to Cuba and the "colonization" of that country by the Soviets are similar to the conditions that gave rise originally to the warning by Monroe and they demand a vigorous application of the same warning. He looks for a reassertion of a basic entailed inheritance.*

A Doctrine Relevant Today

It would be difficult to name any individual other than Adlai Stevenson whose presence in Latin America at this time would create more anxiety among those of us who hope for the preservation of long-established and respected national policies. For he and our other foreign-policy administrators may make decisions from day to day which may weaken and abrogate the very principles upon which our national security was established and has since been maintained.

Among those principles in this hemisphere is the Monroe Doctrine, which came into being because of the threat to our security by Russian imperialist aggression. This aggressive tradition remains unchanged.

In 1821 Czar Alexander proclaimed a ukase which forbade any non-Russian navigation and fishing in the waters of the Pacific 100 miles from the North American coast from the Bering Strait to the 51st parallel, in clear violation of international law and custom.

George Canning, the British Foreign Minister, reminded the United States of the joint responsibility of his country and ours. President Monroe took counsel with Jefferson and Madison, and with Secretary of State John Quincy Adams composed the famous statement. The Monroe Doctrine was aimed at Russia and its partners in the Holy Alliance, Prussia and Austria.

It said that "the American continents

---

* Raymond Moley, "Perspective," in *Newsweek*. Copyright June 26, 1961, and September 24, 1962, by Newsweek, Inc. Reprinted with the permission of *Newsweek*.

... shall henceforth not be considered as subjects for future colonization by any European power."

Alien Systems

Then, recognizing that the unholy trinity had designs to move in on the new Latin American states lately freed from Spanish rule, it declared:

"The political system of the allied powers is essentially different . . . from that of America . . . we should consider any attempt on their part to extend their system to any part of this hemisphere as dangerous to our peace and security."

Those great Secretaries of State and Presidents who reaffirmed the Doctrine in the generations which followed placed its basis firmly, as Secretary Elihu Root said 80 years later, "upon the right of self protection, and that right is recognized by international law." It was, moreover, accepted in the stipulation accepted by the nations subscribing to the Hague conventions of 1899 and 1907, in these words: "Nor shall anything contained in the said convention be construed to imply a relinquishment by the United States of America of its traditional attitude toward purely American questions."

Heirs to a Principle

A century after the announcement of the Doctrine, one of our most eminent Secretaries of State, Charles Evans Hughes—who, it should be noted, through continuing non-recognition of Soviet Russia pointed to the essentially malign nature of Communism—stated the modern meaning of the Monroe Doctrine:

"It still remains, to be applied if necessary, as a principle of national security. Its significance lies in the fact that, in its essentials as set forth by President Monroe and as forcibly asserted by responsible statesmen, it has been for 100 years, and continues to be, an integral part of national thought and purpose expressing a profound conviction which even the upheaval caused by the world war, and the participation of the United States in that struggle on European soil, did not upset."

At this moment it should be underlined that the Doctrine applies not just to the acquisition of territory, but to the extension of a "system." (And Communism is more inimical than was the Holy Alliance.) Now there is not merely a threat but an actual, demonstrable fact that the Communist system is established in Cuba and in strong Communist movements in other Latin American nations.

The men selected by the President to interpret foreign policy are the heirs of a principle established and maintained by illustrious American statesmen. The Monroe Doctrine is an "entailed" inheritance. It cannot be sold for the promise of good will nor given away, nor dissipated by reinterpretation. Those who speak for the nation now are not creators, they are trustees.

* * *

In a characteristic campaign outburst, Harry S. Truman said two weeks ago: "The reason we're in trouble in Cuba is that Ike didn't have the guts to enforce the Monroe Doctrine." It will serve no purpose in the crisis that we face in Cuba to reply that until Castro had deliberately proclaimed himself to be a Communist any application of the Monroe Doctrine would have been quite inappropriate. It is true that Castro's allegiance to the Communist system should have been known to the Eisenhower Administration well before he gained undisputed control of the island republic. Our two ambasadors there learned about it, but were not permitted by the State Department bureaucracy to tell their story to Secretary Dulles and President Eisenhower. But even then it would have been difficult legally to sustain the assertion that an alien system had been imposed from without. The Soviet take-over has been consummated since President Eisenhower left the White House.

Without in any way presenting an excuse for the paralysis which has characterized the Kennedy Administration since the Bay of Pigs affair, a number of considerations qualify the direct application of the doctrine proclaimed nearly 140 years ago.

Changed Conditions

My space here does not permit a detailed account of the nature and various applications of the principle established by President Monroe and his Secretary of State, John Quincy Adams. The reader is referred to the easily accessible and brilliant article by Charles Evans Hughes in the Encyclopaedia Britannica.

A considerable number of Americans believe, with Khrushchev, that the Monroe Doctrine is dead. This belief is based upon several developments since World War I.

The Monroe Doctrine asserted this as a major premise: "In the wars of the European powers in matters relating to themselves we have never taken a part, nor does it comport with our policy so to do." The argument follows that we have within half a century participated in two European wars and that, as the aftermath of the most recent one, we have powerful military installations in Europe designed not only to protect Europe from Soviet aggression but also to serve as a means of defending the United States itself.

Another point urged against the unilateral application of the Monroe Doctrine to Cuba is that we have involved ourselves in treaties and other obligations which act as legal restraints—NATO, the Organization of American States, and also the United Nations. In the light of these changed conditions, it is suggested that in our efforts to establish collective security we have seriously exposed our own security as a sovereign state.

Living Principles

These considerations are, of course, well known to the Soviet, and that is why they can act so boldly in their Cuban take-over. They also realize that our Anglo-American heritage forces us to provide plausible legal justifications for every move we make to protect our security and interests. The Soviet, like the Nazi regime, and even the German Empire which invaded Belgium in World War I, have not been bound by a respect for law.

In replying to the assertion that the Monroe Doctrine is dead, several vital points can be made. One is that the Monroe Doctrine specifically said that we should regard as an unfriendly act any further colonization in the New World; also, that we should resist any introduction of an alien "system" in this hemisphere. We have repeatedly denied our desire for territorial gain, nor do we have any intention to colonize anywhere. Our basis in Turkey and Spain have nothing to do with the internal affairs of those nations. The Communist take-over in Cuba is a barefaced operation designed to establish a Communist- and Soviet-dominated state in the center of the Western Hemisphere.

Suggestions for Further Reading

Because the purpose of this pamphlet is to acquaint the student with the various aspects of a historical problem, the suggestions for further reading include not only books and articles but sources as well. The sources are important because they permit the student to see for himself the raw materials, draw his own conclusions, make his own interpretations, and evaluate the use made of the documentary evidence by the authors of the books and articles.

The principal sources in print for a study of the Monroe Doctrine are the diplomatic correspondence of the United States, Great Britain, and Russia, and the private letters and papers of the chief participants. The official American correspondence is in *American State Papers, Class I, Foreign Relations, 1789–1828* (6 vols., Washington, 1832–1859) and W. R. Manning, *Diplomatic Correspondence of the United States concerning the Independence of the Latin-American Nations* (3 vols., New York, 1925). For Great Britain, the student should see the appropriate volumes in the great collection of *British and Foreign States Papers, 1812–1929* (London, 1941—in progress) and C. K. Webster (ed.), *Britain and the Independence of Latin-America 1810–1830* (2 vols., London, 1938); for Russia, there is "Correspondence of the Russian Ministers in Washington, 1818–1825," in *American Historical Review, XVIII* (1913), 309–345, 537–562.

The printed collections of the letters and papers of individuals contain much official correspondence. But more important, they reveal thoughts, feelings, and opinions that explain much of why things happened and how decisions were made. For the American side, the *Memoirs of John Quincy Adams, 1795—1848*, edited by C. F. Adams (12 vols., Philadelphia, 1874–1877) and the *Writings of John Quincy Adams [1779–1823]*, edited by W. C. Ford (7 vols., New York, 1913–1917) are indispensable. Adams, as secretary of state, was more deeply involved in the diplomatic maneuverings of the period than any other single person. Of great importance, naturally, are President Monroe's Papers collected by S. M. Hamilton as *The Writings of James Monroe* (7 vols., New York, 1898–1903). The American minister in London, Richard Rush, had a great influence on the policy makers in Washington. His reports to the President and to the Secretary of State analyzed the British position and reported generally on the European situation. Hence, his *Memoranda of a Residence at the Court of London . . . from 1819 to 1825* (Philadelphia, 1845) is of the highest significance. In A. A. Lipscomb and A. E. Bergh, *The Writings of Thomas Jefferson* (20 vols., Washington, 1903–1904), Henry Adams, *The Writings of Albert Gallatin* (3 vols., Philadelphia, 1879), and Calvin Colton, *Works of Henry Clay* (6 vols., New York, 1863; vol. 7, 1897) valuable insights may be gleaned. Gallatin served as minister to France; Jefferson was called upon by Monroe for advice; and Clay, as an important political figure, had discussions and corresponded with all the notables of the day.

George Canning's role may be assessed first hand by reference to E. J, Stapleton, *Some Official Correspondence of George Canning* (2 vols., London, 1887). Important background material may be found in Charles Vane, *Correspondence, Despatches, and Other Papers* [*of Viscount Castlereagh*] (12 vols., London, 1848–1853.). Castlereagh was Canning's predecessor in the foreign office and was instrumental in setting Britain's course in relation to the revolutions in South America and to the alliance system on the Continent. The French minister in Washington, Guillaume Hyde de Neuville, has left *Memoires et Souvenirs du Baron Hyde de Neuville* (3 vols., Paris, 1912) and the French Prime Minister, Count Jean Baptiste de Villèle, has collected his *Memoires et Correspondance* (5 vols., Paris, 1888–1890). Both contain interesting and valuable material on the French position.

As for books and articles, Dexter Perkins, *The Monroe Doctrine, 1823–1826* (Cambridge, Mass., 1927) contains an excellent bibliography. Additional listings may be found in H. H. B. Meyer, *List of References on the Monroe Doctrine* (Washington, 1919) and Phillips Bradley, *A Bibliography of the Monroe Doctrine, 1919–1929* (London, 1929).

The starting point of any study of the Doctrine is Dexter Perkins' volume mentioned above. It is multiarchival, thorough, intensive, and complete in research. It may be supplemented by two additional studies in which Perkins carries the story of the Doctrine to 1907: *The Monroe Doctrine, 1826–1867* (Baltimore, 1933) and *The Monroe Doctrine, 1867–1907* (Baltimore, 1937). In 1941, he incorporated his vast and unmatched knowledge of the subject in a single volume, *Hands Off: A History of the Monroe Doctrine* (Boston, 1941 and also in paperback revised edition, 1955). As indicated by the selections in this pamphlet, Perkins must be read in conjunction with Edward H. Tatum, Jr., and Arthur P. Whitaker. It would be instructive to read, in addition, Georg Heinz, *Die Beziehungen zwischen Russland, England, und Nordamerika in Jahre 1823* (Berlin, 1911), one of the earliest works emphasizing the problem of Cuba and Anglo-American rivalry as the basis for Monroe's pronouncement. A similar approach is taken by J. Fred Rippy, *Rivalry of the United States and Great Britain over Latin-America, 1808–1830* (Baltimore, 1929). There are four early studies which presage Perkins' point of view: A. B. Hart, *The Monroe Doctrine: an Interpretation* (Boston, 1916), G. F. Tucker, *The Monroe Doctrine: A Concise History of Its Origin and Growth* (Boston, 1885), W. F. Reddaway, *The Monroe Doctrine* (New York, 1905), and T. B. Edgington, *The Monroe Doctrine* (Boston, 1904).

For the European background of events which affected the Western Hemisphere, W. P. Cresson, *The Holy Alliance: The European Background of the Monroe Doctrine* (New York, 1922) and W. A. Phillips, *The Confederation of Europe: A Study of the European Alliance, 1813–1823* (London and New York, 1920) are adequate. C. K. Webster, *The Foreign Policy of Castlereagh, 1815–1822* (London, 1925) is excellent. It describes Britain's relations to the Continental powers and to their plans for suppressing rebellion in the Old World and in the New.

For the immediate events preceding the statement by Monroe, the British side of the story is covered with accuracy, thoroughness, and objectivity by H. W. V. Temperley, *The Foreign Policy of Canning, 1822–1827* (London, 1925). Volume two of the *Cambridge History of British Foreign Policy* (3 vols., Cambridge, 1922–1923) is also valuable. William W. Kaufmann's book, *British Policy and Latin America* (New Haven, Conn., 1951), from which a selection is reprinted in this pamphlet, may be read in its entirety with profit. It is the most recent work of scholarship on the subject. Stanley Lane-Pool, *The Life of the Right Honorable Stratford Canning* (2 vols., London and New York, 1888) is a judicious biography of George Canning's cousin, the British minister in Washington. French policy is the subject of W. S. Robertson, *France and Latin-American Independence* (Baltimore, 1939).

Accounts of the Monroe Administration and biographies of Monroe are not numerous. The Dangerfield book is the only good narrative of Monroe's presidency. There is no first-rate biography of the fifth president, but W. P. Cresson, *James Monre* (Chapel Hill, N.C., 1946) is adequate. D. C. Gilman, *James Monroe* (New York, 1890) while old is still very much worth reading. For John Quincy Adams, Samuel F. Bemis, *John Quincy Adams and the Foundations of American Foreign Policy* (New York, 1949) is the best and only book worth reading. Bemis' admiration for his subject does not mar the prodigious scholarship of the work or the thoughtfulness of the narrative. It is superior biography and diplomatic history, and provides a stimulating account of the events leading to the promulgation of the Doctrine as seen by one of the principal participants. Another important biography is J. H. Powell, *Richard Rush: Republican Diplomat* (Philadelphia, 1942) in which the Rush-Canning conversations are described.

Two articles by W. S. Roberston discuss the effect of the Doctrine: "The Monroe Doctrine Abroad, 1823–1824," *American Political Science Review*, VI (1912), 546–563, describes the reception in England, France, Spain, and Austria, and "South America and the Monroe Doctrine, 1824–1828," *Political Science Quarterly*, XXX (1915), 82–105, analyzes the reaction in Colombia, Brazil, and the provinces of the Río de la Plata. Laura Bornholdt adds additional information on the Abbé de Pradt's contribution to the ideas of the Doctrine in "The Abbé de Pradt and the Monroe Doctrine," *Hispanic American Historical Review*, 24 (1944), 201–221. T. B. Davis, Jr., does the same for Carlos de Alvear in "Carlos de Alvear and James Monroe: New Light on the origin of the Monroe Doctrine," *Hispanic American Historical Review*, 23 (1943), 632–649. For United States relations with Russia and the crisis arising out of that power's expansion on the west coast of North America, see J. C. Hildt, *Early Diplomatic Relations of the United States and Russia* (Baltimore, 1906).

The literature concerning the corollaries that have been added to the original Monroe Doctrine is very extensive. John A. Logan, *No Transfer* (New Haven, Conn., 1961) deals historically with the question of the nontransference of territory in the Western Hemisphere from one non-American power to another. G. B. Young, "Intervention Under the Monroe Doctrine: the Olney Corollary," *Political Science Quarterly*, LVII (1942), 247–280, discusses the intervention of the United States in the British-Venezuelan boundary dispute as an extension of the Monroe Doctrine. The attempt to extend the Doctrine to interference in this hemisphere by an Asiatic nation is examined by Thomas A. Bailey, "The Lodge Corollary to the Monroe Doctrine," *Political Science Quarterly*, XLVIII (1933), 220–239.

The most significant corollary attached to the Doctrine is the one announced by President Theodore Roosevelt in 1905. Its origin and development may be traced in H. C. Hill, *Roosevelt and the Caribbean* (Chicago, 1937), H. K. Beale, *Theodore Roosevelt and the Rise of America to World Power* (Baltimore, 1956), and J. F. Rippy, "Antecedents of the Roosevelt Corollary of the Monroe Doctrine," *Pacific Historical Review*, IX (1940), 267–279. Of great importance to an understanding of the Roosevelt Corollary is J. R. Clark, *Memorandum on the Monroe Doctrine* (Washington, 1930) in which an undersecretary of state disassociated American intervention from the Monroe Doctrine and repudiated Roosevelt's corollary.

There are two essays which relate the Doctrine to World War II: F. O. Wilcox, "The Monroe Doctrine and World War II," *American Political Science Review*, XXXVI (1942), 433–453, and Dexter Perkins, "Bringing the Monroe Doctrine Up to Date," *Foreign Affairs* XX (1942), 253–265.